LULU H

(THE GEORGIA WONDER,)

WRITES HER AUTOBIOGRAPHY,

AND FOR THE FIRST TIME

EXPLAINS AND DEMONSTRATES

THE

GREAT SECRET

OF

HER MARVELOUS POWER.

WHO READS THE BOOK CAN ACQUIRE THE POWER.

WITH A FOREWORD BY
BOB FRIEDHOFFER

LULU HURST BOOK CO., PUBLISHERS.
Order and Mailing Department: ROME, GA.
Agency and Shipping Department: MADISON, GA.
1897.

LULU HURST, ("THE GEORGIA WONDER,")
NOW MRS. PAUL ATKINSON.

I DEDICATE THIS BOOK TO MY

Beloved Parents and My Husband,

(who was my Manager on the stage,)

AND ALSO TO MY DEAR FRIENDS OF BEAUTIFUL CEDAR
VALLEY, ALL OF WHOM WERE MOST STEADFAST
AND ENTHUSIASTIC BELIEVERS IN THE
OCCULT NATURE OF "THE GREAT
UNKNOWN POWER."

THE AUTHOR.

LULU HURST,

(THE GEORGIA WONDER,)

FOREWORD.

THE Georgia Wonder was a national phenomenon.

Lulu Hurst's teenage performances in the 1880s were written up in newspapers, scientific journals and magazines of all sorts.

A slight girl, she would stand on stage and challenge men to lift her off of the ground. At one moment a large man could raise her from the stage and at the next would find himself powerless to do so. It was as if she controlled gravity.

Another stunt was to stand while holding a pool cue horizontally in front of her and have a number of men push against her. They were unable to push her off her spot.

Yet another stunt was to have three men sit on a chair and the apparently lift the chair and men from the ground.

This autobiography, chronicles her life, culminating in an exposé of how she performed her feats.

This book will interest: magicians, scientists in general, physicists in particular, feminists, those who follow the occult arts, and readers who would like to glimpse a life led by a teenage girl in the late 1800s.

–Bob Friedhoffer

INTRODUCTION.

Who is Lulu Hurst? What is the Georgia Wonder?

Ask any one you chance to meet on the street, in the train or on the roadside, and they will tell you that a few years ago she, a 14-year-old girl, startled and mystified the American continent as no living mortal ever did before, or ever can do again.

She flashed athwart the sky of this continent like some weird, supernal meteor, whose nature and mission no one could divine, and, having overwhelmed this hemisphere with consternation and mystery, she suddenly disappeared from the wondering gaze of all, leaving no light behind her to illumine the deep, dark secret of her marvelous power! She baffled all scientists and dismayed all skeptics! She exhibited "Forces" and performed marvels that the wisest and most conservative men pronounced supernatural and miraculous. College professors, doctors, scientific investigators, common sense business men, one and all pronounced her wonderful "Force" and its phenomena to be inexplicable and unfathomable.

For two years or more she astonished the nation, and then disappeared as suddenly as she had come.

The Press of the Continent Wrote Thousands of Columns About Her.

While she was before the public, the newspapers and journals and magazines published more about her in the length of time than was ever devoted to any other personage of this country.

Why Did She Disappear so Suddenly?

Why did she abandon the stage where money was flowing into her coffers as water into a whirlpool, and where people by the tens of thousands flocked to see her and pay tribute to the exhibition of her "Great Unknown Power"? What became of her after she left the stage? Into what secret abiding place did she carry "The Great Secret"? Has she done anything toward solving the dark problem of the mysterious "Force"? What was and is the destiny of this strange "Force," which was so miraculously associated with the person of this 14-year-old girl? What strange and exciting incidents happened to her during her early life, and while she was on the stage?

The remarkable book written by her answers all these questions and explains the Great Secret of her life and "Power."

It is stranger than any "Arabian Nights' Tales" ever written, and every word recorded in its stirring pages is the truth. The inspired fancy and wild imagination of a Jules Verne, Eugene Sue or Victor Hugo would be impotent to conceive a tale so weird and wonderful as this narrative of facts and truths unfolds.

Its pages are alive with stirring scenes and exciting incidents, and in every chapter is a strange, attractive mixture of mystery and fun.

In addition to the vivid accounts of these stirring, realistic and wonderful scenes that occurred on the stage and in public and private, the author details many experiences she had with eminent people all over the continent, gives their views of, and experiences with, the "Great Unknown Power," and tells how they acted when under its "influence." Throughout the book is a commingling of the sad, the ludicrous, the exciting and the tragic. It will afford a mine of thought to scientists and savants.

In Part II. of the volume is given a full and complete explanation of the "Great Secret" of these forces.

The author tells how she began to study her "Power" after leaving the stage, and how she has kept up her investigations during the years since, until finally she solved the problem which had baffled the minds of the greatest thinkers of the continent. She demonstrates the nature, mode of action and application of these "Forces," and gives the underlying reason and *modus operandi* of every "Test" she performed on the stage, so that every one can fully understand the "Great Mystery," and accomplish the same feats exhibited by her.

She illustrates every " Test " with full page Half Tones, showing scientifically how every one of these feats and marvelous exhibitions of power was performed by her, and can be accomplished by all.

The book is a commentary on Human Nature that will be lasting and far-reaching in its effects. It will prove a bulwark to the human reason that is unparalleled in the history of literature. It will strengthen the minds of thousands of people on lines where they need toning up very much. The reason for such a volume as this was never greater than at this time. We present it to the public with full assurance of the useful mission it is bound to fulfil, which the author had in view in writing it.

The work will prove a death-blow to Spiritualism and Superstition of every kind.

THE LULU HURST BOOK COMPANY.

TABLE OF CONTENTS.

PART I.

PART II.

ILLUSTRATIONS

PART I.

CHAPTER I.

A LITTLE CHILDHOOD HISTORY.

The Purpose and Plan of the Book—The Prelude to Wonders More Weird than the Wildest Creations of the Brain of Jules Verne.

To accomplish the purpose I have in view in this book, I think it best in the first part of the volume, to give an account of all occurrences just as they took place, and to recite them in the same environment of mystery in which they appeared to all those who witnessed them, and as they largely appeared to me as a child. Then in the second part of the book I will make an explanation of the "MYSTERIOUS FORCE" which so astonished and mystified the entire public, and *demonstrate* the fact that I have at last succeeded in unraveling and solving the "GREAT SECRET."

To accomplish this end to the satisfaction of every thinking man and woman, I will make an

ABSOLUTE SCIENTIFIC DEMONSTRATION

of each one of the tests separately, so that any one can accomplish them. However, before beginning with the recital of these things, it is necessary to say a little about myself as I now view myself when, at the age of fourteen years, the Wonders related in this book began, and also a little about my family history and the surroundings of my childhood, points about which many people have inquired of me.

I cannot say that my life differed materially from that of other children reared in the country.

I always enjoyed excellent health, was naturally a robust child, happy and rollicking, full of life and spirit.

My father, Mr. W. E. Hurst, enlisted in the Confederate army at the age of seventeen. He was engaged in many battles during the war, and won quite a reputation as a man of bravery and daring. He was an officer in the Reserve Artillery of the Army of Tennessee. He was shot from his horse at the battle of Murfreesboro, and desperately wounded.

Quite a strange coincidence occurred in Atlanta. To tell it, I must go back a little. My father's family were Tennesseeans. As everybody knows, this State was badly divided on the issues of the war of Secession. Father was against son, and brother against brother. So it was in our family. My uncle enlisted in the Federal army and my father, as before stated, in the Confederate. So events led up to the battle of Atlanta on the 22d of July, 1864. In this fight my uncle, fighting in the Federal army, was captured by my father's own company and brought face to face with him. A touching scene ensued, but under the existing state of affairs my uncle had to be carried a prisoner to Andersonville.

When the arbitrament of war had forced a surrender upon the boys in gray, my father returned to Athens, Tenn., his former home, and found everything in ashes and ruin. After a short while he came to Georgia and settled in Polk county, in the beautiful Cedar Valley near Cedartown. Here he married my mother, a daughter of Rev. W. P. Wood and niece of Rev. Jesse Wood. Both of these men were zealous ministers of the Baptist church and beloved throughout Georgia.

Rev. Jesse Wood was at that time President of Woodland Female College in Cedar Valley. I was born in 1869, and in this lovely valley I was reared. Nothing of unusual interest occurred in my early childhood. My father's farm was two miles from Cedartown and there I lived until I was ten years old. I did not attend the neighboring school, but was taught at home by my mother. She was a very intelligent woman, being an alumna of the famous " Mary Sharp College " at Winchester, Tenn.

In the year 1880, when I was eleven years old, my father moved to Cedartown to send myself and brother to school. My teacher at this school was Professor J. C. Harris, now Superintendent of the Public Schools of Rome, Ga. He was my first teacher, and I loved him devotedly. I hope I can still count him as one of my best friends, for I look back with sweet memory upon the school-days of my childhood spent under his tutelage.

We remained in Cedartown only a short time. My

father bought the O. B. Whatley homestead about five miles from Cedartown and we moved there. This was the most beautiful place in that section, quaint and picturesque in all its surroundings. I attended the neighborhood school there taught by my uncle, Clarence Wood. It was in this quaint old homestead that the wonderful phenomena and mysterious "Forces" related in this book began to be manifested. Here about this time occurred manifestations which led on to results that could not have been foretold by a stretch of the wildest imagination on earth.

Should I write a dozen volumes the size of this I could not narrate, and give the published accounts of, all the wonders that occurred in connection with me over this continent, which had their beginning at this time and place.

The record of these things is varied and voluminous. I will only quote enough from the vast mass of published accounts at hand to corroborate and, if need be, verify the statements I make.

CHAPTER II.

A TRUE AND ACCURATE ACCOUNT OF THE
FIRST MANIFESTATION AND THE SUBSE-
QUENT DEVELOPMENT OF MY WONDERFUL
POWER.

*A Night of Storm, Terror, and Mystery—The Neighbors
Called in—The Invisible "It" a Mind-reader.*

By the merest, most trifling accident, I discovered the
beginning of my "Force," by the manifestation of which
I afterwards become famous as an occult prodigy, weird
and wonderful. What that accident was that told the beginning of such marvelous facts as this book will narrate,
I will disclose later on in the proper place. It shows how
our destinies may be determined by the most trifling thing.
I will write here exactly what occurred.

We were now living, as before stated, at our country
place, about five miles from Cedartown. The time was
the night of the 18th day of September, 1883. It was a
very dark night and an electric storm was raging without.
I had retired for the night, and with me was my cousin,
Miss Lora Wimberly, who was visiting us. She was considerably older than myself, but I was very fond of her,
and loved so much to have her stay with me. She was a
young lady of excellent education and accomplished in dif-

ferent branches of art, and she was highly respected and beloved by all who knew her. Her family is one of the best of the State.

I remember very distinctly that the storm this night was a very severe one, and I was in much fear on account of it, and lay awake. My cousin had about gotten to sleep, when we were startled by a quick, muffled, popping sound that, on the instant, seemed to come from anywhere or nowhere.

We jumped up in bed, and she gasped out to me, "What was that?" I told her I did not know. We got up and made a thorough search for big, horny bugs, snakes, etc., but found nothing. We then lay down again. But no sooner were we quiet than the same peculiar, harrowing, muffled, popping noise began again. We now located the sounds more directly under our pillows. We became much alarmed, and the older members of the household were aroused. They came in and helped to search for the cause of these mysterious sounds. The bedding was removed, including the mattress. Everything was turned inside out, but all to no purpose. The mystery grew greater and greater. Every one in the house now became alarmed. A conference was held and it was decided, on the suggestion of my mother, that the sounds were caused by electricity. On this night the atmosphere was surcharged with electricity on account of the severe storm, and all agreed that there could be no solution but that. The household sat up, and the peculiar noise kept up for several hours. After awhile, being partly satisfied that the phenomenon was caused by the storm and would subside with it, the family went off to sleep. The next day nothing was discussed except the mysterious phenomena of the previous night. It was told throughout the neighborhood, and created quite a great sensation. The night following was a beautiful, Southern, autumnal night. After we had retired the noises of the previous night began again, but in a more boisterous form, popping and thumping in the feather bed, then on and in the wood of the footboard, and then, finally, in all parts of the bed. It became alarming. It must be traced to some cause, thought the family, but to what, no one could say. It was decided to arouse the neighbors, and get their assistance in unraveling this mystery. The truth is, the whole family had become terrified. My father, who was as brave a soldier as ever lived, when in the presence of a visible enemy, had become completely demoralized in the presence of this invisible, gruesome mystery. So we decided to call some of the neighbors, and did summon about twenty of them. They assembled and arranged themselves around the room, and listened to these peculiar sounds. All became convinced that they were in the presence of some mysterious force, and it was a sight never to be forgotten, to see the expressions of the different faces assembled there that memorable night. Finally, different ones began to make suggestions. Some thought it was the manifestation of departed or disembodied spirits. Others thought, it could be explained on more rational grounds. Some one suggested that it might be an intelligent force. So, some of the crowd began to ask "it" questions. Among others present at this time was Mr. Fulton Colville, who then lived at Cedartown, but is now one of the most popular leaders among the young men of Atlanta, and a lawyer of great ability.

He asked "it" to tell him the time by his watch. The bed began to "pop," and popped ten times. He then asked it to rap his age, and, as he counted, it rapped twenty-five times, which, he said, was correct. Hundreds of questions were asked and answered in this way. The old bed seemed to be educated. People began to marvel and be afraid, and seemed bereft of all reason. Looking upon the surface of things as we did, we saw or heard the operation of an invisible "Force," which, intangible and unseen, acted upon matter, and in all of its manifestations, showed not only intelligence, but a species of mind-reading that would have dumbfounded the learned members of "The Society of Psychical Research."

CHAPTER III.

THE WONDERS GREW—STILL MORE MARVELOUS MANIFESTATIONS IN THE "HAUNTED HOUSE" OF CEDAR VALLEY.

Wrestling with Mystery—Mysterious Movement of Objects— All Natural Laws Seemingly Set Aside.

Within a week from the beginning of the action of the "Force," as narrated in the previous chapter, the manifestations had become tenfold more wonderful. While many people were actually afraid to approach the "Haunted House," as our house was now called, yet the curiosity of a great many got the best of them, and our home was overrun. We had to improvise beds of all sorts for the crowds to sleep on, many coming from adjoining counties.

I will now tell of some of the more remarkable phenomena that had aroused the public interest to such a pitch of excitement.

Following the mysterious "rapping" in and on the bed, some one had suggested that several of us join, or place, our hands on a table. There being no table in the room at the time I speak of, we placed our hands on a chair. Everybody was excited and wrought up to a high pitch. The chair began to quiver and tremble, and then commenced to gyrate about the room. Life seemed to have gotten into the chair. The question now came up, was this force associated with any particular person? Was there any one present who controlled this peculiar influence? It was found, upon investigation, that it followed me. The "Force" seemed to take possession of objects when my hands, *in conjunction with others,* came in contact with them.

The settlement of this point led on to various experiments with me. When I placed my hands upon a chair which was held firmly by another person, or any number of persons, it became uncontrollable. I well remember the intense excitement connected with the first effort to hold the chair. Several strong young men attempted to hold it with my hands upon it. They tore that chair rung from rung and post from pillar trying to hold it. They swung all their weight on it, they braced against it,—they pulled off their coats and wrestled with the "Unknown Power";—in their struggles they crashed the mirrors and the lamps in the room, they defaced the walls, and broke the doors from the hinges. They declared they were shocked as by some electric current. After the struggle some of them were so bruised and exhausted that they had to be "doctored" and rubbed. The next day several of them were in bed from fright and over-exertion.

Be it distinctly understood that during a great part of the time, this our first desperate struggle with a chair was taking place, *my hands were not touching the chair.* I was standing aside witnessing the wonderful performance, as were the other spectators, and was, of course, greatly astonished. The suggestion was made that we try the "Force" with a cane. No one could hold the cane, or keep on his feet in any position of steadiness, when I touched it. We tried it with as many strong men as could get hold of it. The number or strength of the men made no difference. We tried the "Force" on an open umbrella, the test being for any one to hold it when I put my hands on the handle of it. The result was the same as in the test with the chair and the cane. No one could hold it; and in the struggle the umbrella was torn to pieces and turned inside out.

My father and mother, however, resented the idea that this force was associated with me any more than any one else. They tried to persuade me from entertaining any such an idea. They greatly feared it would have a bad effect on my mind and nervous system, for I was but a fourteen-year-old child. Still I knew they suspected me as being the subject through whom the force operated. I would catch them watching me, as they feared the force would do me harm. During the night they often visited my room and sat for hours about my bed, when I was asleep. About this time some other strange things happened which increased their anxiety about me still more, and which aroused the community to a more violent pitch of excitement, if that were possible. My cousin, Miss Lora Wimberly, who, as I before stated, was on a visit to us, was packing her trunk to go home. Having packed the most of her clothes in the trunk, she noticed that certain garments disappeared therefrom without her knowledge of how or when they went. She came in the other room where my mother was, to tell her about it, and while doing so, lo! before her very eyes, and the eyes of others in the room, one of the missing garments was seen to pass through the air, and alight on a picture hanging on the wall.

We screamed with terror and all rushed from the room. At the time this strange thing happened, the doors and windows of the room were closed. Others of her garments were found in other rooms of the house, where it was thought they had been mysteriously placed.

On the mantel of one of the rooms where we were sitting, my father had placed some rocks and pebbles, specimens of certain ores found on his lands. While we would be sitting in this room, or even in other parts of the house, these pebbles would fly through the air and fall upon the floor about us, and sometime strike us in falling.

At other times particles of sulphur were seen to fall about on the floor. A tumbler, on one occasion, rolled violently down the hall and broke into fragments. These, and other similar remarkable phenomena, were occurring at different times. My father became more and more uneasy, not only concerning my safety, but the safety of his personal property. He took all his jewelry and valuable papers to Cedartown and stored them there for safe-keeping. He was afraid the "Power" would spirit them away. I pacified him by telling him that I believed if the "Power" could take away things, it could bring them back, and that I thought it would do us no harm. All this time my self-possession and calmness, which was always remarkable for a child, did more to keep down the excitement than anything else. Had I given way to fear or superstitious belief, matters would have indeed been desperate with us. In fact, my father had made up his mind to leave our home and go elsewhere, but I told him the probability was the "Power" would follow us there, and we would find things no better. He yielded to this view and did not move. Remember, all these things occurred during the same week that the manifestations began. One night, during the latter part of this week, my cousin and I had gone to bed. We were not quite asleep when suddenly I felt some one pull my hair, and I, thinking, of course, it was my cousin, asked her why she had done it. She replied that she had not touched it. It then occurred to me that it was the work of the "Power," and I so suggested to her, and this alarmed her beyond endurance. She shrieked for my father, and rushed from the room. His alarm at this was fearful. He came at a bound into the room with a heavy chair in position to strike down any vile intruder, but none could be found. This justified his fears that this "power" or "force" would do me harm in some way, or perhaps carry me away. On this night we sat up till morning, fearing another and a more violent attack of some sort. After this, a closer watch was kept on me than ever to insure my protection and safety. While these mysterious things were taking place in the house, other strange phenomena, operating from without, were occurring. Just in front about twenty steps a little to one side of our house, was a large hickory nut tree, which at this time was laden with nuts, just ripening and beginning to fall. These nuts would fly into the room and scatter over the floor, and often strike members of the family in passing through the air. They would apparently fly through the window. Even at times when the windows were down, these nuts would be hurled through the air into the room, coming from points and entering the room, no one knew where. This phenomenon increased the terror of the family and neighbors very much. This tree soon came to be called the "Electrical Hickory Nut Tree," and is so designated to-day. This tree can be seen in the cut of the "haunted house" on the back of this volume. When the strange phenomena connected with it were occurring, everybody had a superstitious awe about it, and looked upon its stately form with anything but pleasant sensations.

During this excitement, among a great number who came out to our home to see and test the Power, I can recall the following persons: Professor J. C. Harris of Cedartown, a very prominent educator; Mrs. Ida Hardwick, wife of the president of the Cedartown bank; Mr. A. D. Hogg, member of the Georgia legislature; Mr. D. B. Freeman, editor of the Cedartown *Advertiser;* Mr. Fulton Colville, a prominent lawyer of Atlanta; Mr. John Dodds, an enterprising business man of Cedartown; Mr. W. C. Bunn, mayor of Cedartown; Mr. Jim Lampton, real estate broker of Washington, D. C., with hundreds of others. Reporters of the papers began to arrive to write up matters concerning the " Wonderful Lulu Hurst."

The following newspaper account of these Wonders was written by Mr. D. B. Freeman, and published at the time in the Cedartown *Advertiser*, and gave wide circulation to these wonderful happenings. I give it here as a sample of many others that appeared about that time, reporters from Rome, Cartersville, Atlanta, and other points visiting our home and writing up the Wonderful Manifestations. Some of these articles will be reproduced later on in the book; but this one will suffice at present. The article is as follows:

"In a recent issue of the *Advertiser* we gave an account of the visit to the home of Mr. Wm. E. Hurst, in this county, for the purpose of witnessing the reported extraordinary and inexplicable power possessed by his daughter, Miss Lulu. We told what our eyes had witnessed—how that, by the touch of her hands, a chair or other objects became violently restless and ungovernable. We have reports now of mysterious manifestations about the Hurst household beside which those previously told smack of rather the diminutive wonder. We would be slow to record a statement of these mysterious occurrences, if we were not assured of their truthfulness by as respectable and trustworthy people as dwell in our whole section, including members of the family, her cousin, Miss Wimberly, and her uncle, Mr. Clarence Wood.

"Miss Wimberly is the constant roommate of Miss Lulu. She missed a garment from among her clothing, and supposed it to be stolen. A number of other garments were subsequently missed, the disappearance of which could not be reasonably accounted for. Finally, Miss Wimberly looked for some garments, she had just placed in a trunk among some other clothing and securely shut the lid. No human hand having been about the trunk since she had placed it there, she was naturally much mystified. Wondering in their own minds in what new way their visions would be startled and their reasons taxed, the members of the household were taken severely aback by the discovery by some one of a missing handkerchief hanging over a picture in the room. This might be accounted for by attributing its appearance there to some unknown human hand, and the members of the household so believe, and all leaving the room, securely locked it. Returning very soon another missed garment is seen hanging from the

cornice of the window. Three persons sit in the room,
and instantly appears before their vision a missing garment
hanging over the head-board of the bed. Another garment,
not missed but instantly recognized, appears on a picture
in the room. A hat known to have been placed in a
bureau drawer in one room, is found in a careless position
in a closet in another room across the hall. Some small
mineral specimens which had been placed on a mantel in
the room they occupy are scattered over the floor, startling
the senses of those who observe them. On an evening
embraced in the period covering these manifestations,
members of the family while sitting in another room heard
a noise in the hall. They entered it and observed a tumbler,
which had been left on the dining room table, lying in a
corner as if forcibly hurled by some hand. Other minor
experiences of a mysterious nature have been related to us,
but we will end now with what we have mentioned."

CHAPTER IV.

HOW THE PRESSING DEMAND OF THE PUB-LIC CARRIED ME TO THE STAGE.

My First Public Exhibition—A Crowd Wild with Excite-ment Greets Me—The Power, Like a Mighty Storm, Car-ries Everything before It—Men, Chairs, Canes, and Um-brellas Hurled Into " Confusion Worse Confounded."

When these things were taking place at home and the crowds of people were coming there from the neighborhood and from Cedartown, and even as far off as Rome and At-lanta, we did not dream of making a public exhibition of the "Power" and its wonderful doings.

Such a thing as making money out of it was farthest from our mind.   But hundreds of people came to our home. They urged us to go before the public.   We would not consent.   The truth is, my father being a deacon of the Baptist church of Cedartown, and of the strictest old school style, did not like the idea of any sort of an opera-house or stage performance.   I said to those who came to me and asked me about the "Power," "You see the performance; I can't explain it; judge for yourself."   In the course of a week or ten days our life-long friends from Cedartown came out and begged and insisted that we give a public exhibi-

(17)

tion there. After much persuasion we consented, though my father was never fully reconciled to it.

No one can imagine how much he was opposed to the notoriety the occurrences had caused. But he yielded to the urgent demands of our friends and the public, remembering that we were among our friends and neighbors, and that we could not, under the circumstances, be subjected to any harsh criticism, if the "Power" was a failure before the public.

But I said then and there, "While I will try and give this exhibition here before my relatives and friends, there it must end."

The night of our first public exhibition was auspicious for me, in that the hall where I exhibited was crowded to its utmost capacity. Standing room was at a premium. It was a trying ordeal to me in more ways than one. Here I was, looked upon as the "Wonder" of the age, believed to possess powers allied to the supernatural, if not the miraculous. That crowd expected me to perform miracles. My fame had gone forth in all that region as a Wonder-Worker. Those present, who had seen me before, told everybody what they had seen with their own eyes and heard with their own ears. If there was anything they had really not seen or heard, their imagination came to their aid and supplied the deficiency. So those present, who had not witnessed my "Power," really expected more than the others. They were "seeking for a sign," as it were, from the supernal realms. A young girl, in a short silk frock and blue waist, was expected to set aside the eternal laws of gravitation, reverse the order of nature, paralyze the muscular energy of any number of strong men, and by her touch impart incarnate life to dead matter, such as chairs, tables, canes, umbrellas, etc. I was that girl, and I was there to demonstrate and exemplify this great "Unknown Force." I think I can safely and truly say that no other child in the history of the world ever occupied such a unique position as I did. For the first time since the "Wonders" started with me, I began to realize my position before the world.

At that time my "Tests" were fewer in the illustration and demonstration of the "Force" than I acquired later. But notwithstanding this fact, the audience was as deeply expectant and awe-struck, as if they had come to see me walk upon the water, or fly unaided through the air. Was it not a miracle to reverse the order of nature and set aside its laws? And did not Lulu Hurst do this? Was it not wonderful if she did it with only one test instead of with more? So in these respective attitudes the audience and I faced each other.

My tests then were what is known as "The Umbrella Test"; the attempt of any number of men to hold a chair or cane when I placed my hands on them; and the attempt to put a chair to the floor while I rested my hands on it.

My father was with me on the stage, and invited any number of reputable citizens to come on the stage and test the "Power."

The stage was brightly lighted. Everything was in full view of the audience, and every one in the audience had full confidence in us and in the dozen or more reputable citizens who had come upon the stage. My father stated to the people what I would do, that is, what the tests were. He invited any one on the stage to firmly grasp a strong

cane about five feet long, keep steadily upon his feet, and
hold it when I put my hand on it.   One of the strongest
men on the stage got up, and with the grip of a vise took
hold of the cane with each hand and held it out horizontally
in front of him, bracing himself firmly on his feet. He
held the cane with his hands about two and one half or
three feet apart.   He was cautioned by my father to hold it
firmly, because he was afraid it would fly out of his grasp
and strike me.   I placed one of my hands on the cane,
with the palm against it, about midway between his hands.
It generally required a minute or so for the force to begin
its work.   I stood facing the big man without moving a
muscle.   One of the strange things connected with me, in
making the tests, was that I could not keep from laughing.

I cannot say that my success depended on my laughing,
but any way I always had to laugh just as though it was a necessity to my success, and for this reason many of the newspapers referred to me as "Laughing Lulu Hurst."   Later
on in the book I will tell why I always laughed during
these tests.   As we stood thus, the big man grim and solemn
and an earnestness as of death showing in his face, and
his muscles knotted like corrugated iron, the audience
gazed in breathless silence and in pent-up excitement.
Very soon, perhaps in less time than it takes to tell it, the
big man began to quiver, and then to totter, and then to
brace himself, and then to lose his balance, and then to
dance, and then to jump, and in the next instant he tumbled into a heap in the corner of the stage, knocking over
several dignified citizens in his mad rush and tumble.   To
say that the audience went wild is putting it mildly.   The
house was pandemonium turned loose and upside down.

People stood on the seats and yelled and laughed like mad-men, and threw up their hats and canes regardless of where they fell, or whose head they cracked. The big man who had tested the "Power" was panting like a matador in a Spanish bull fight. He said the "Power" had rendered him powerless for the night.

Then three men attempted, in the same way, to hold the cane. They were arranged along the cane on the opposite side of it from me, as the big man was before. I laughed in their faces and put my hand on the cane, and lo! the "Power" came and—they went; hither and thither they swayed, and bent, and doubled up, and straightened out. They braced, and fell too. They lost their balance, and over they went in a heap one on top of the other. When the cane was examined, it was found to be twisted into pieces by the "Force," and a stout, well-seasoned hickory cane had been used in the test.

Then came one of the tests with the chair. This test was for any person to put the back of the chair to his breast and grasp the front rung on one side and the upright post on the other, and hold the chair steady when I took hold of it. In this test I placed the open palm of one hand on the back of the chair next to the breast of the holder, and the other palm I laid on the front of the seat. The chair used was strongly built out of seasoned oak. It behaved exactly like the cane. The stored up energy of ages of sturdy mountain oaks seemed to be turned loose in it. It seemed to have even inherited the mighty ferocity of the storms, which for ages had battled with its ancestors in the mountain fastnesses of Cedar Valley. The pent-up force of these storms seemed suddenly to come to life in that chair. It rushed forward and then backward. It rocked to and fro as its giant parent in the forest had often done. It leaned forward and then straightened up, always carrying with it the piece of humanity, called a strong man, who was trying to hold it, as though he was but a leaf in the blast of a fierce wind. Suddenly, there was a quick upward and backward movement of the chair, and over upon his head went the exhausted victim.

Then three men attempted to hold it, and though they succeeded in tearing it limb from limb, yet they went down in disaster with it to the floor. It was impossible for them to hold it still, or stay upon their feet. In this way chair after chair was torn to pieces that night, and any number of exhausted men tossed sprawling upon the floor of the stage, as though they were limber-drunk idiots or weak-legged imbeciles.

The next test was for some strong man to take up a chair and hold it firmly to his body, to keep it from flying out and striking me, and then for two, three, five, or more men besides himself, to put the chair to the floor while I had my hand upon it. Here was the same struggle as before. That chair to all appearances rested upon the back of some invisible leviathan. It seemed to ride upon the incompressible air, or on the billows of some invisible ocean of power, like a mighty war-ship in its pride and glory and strength rocks upon the vast deep. True, now and then the chair would descend toward the floor, but before it would go far downward, it would suddenly change its direction and rise upward, as though mounting the crest of a giant wave. It would then bear forward north by east or south by west, carrying its struggling burden along with it, until they were wrecked in some whirlpool, in which the men went down with the chair on top of them. Again and again was this test made by me, and always successfully. At times, in these struggles, *my hands were not even touching the chair,* and yet it was never put to the floor. In every instance every man declared to the audience that he had done his best, and, as he made his solemn statement, he gasped for breath, and wiped the superabundant perspiration from his face. The doctors would examine me and find my pulse and respiration normal, and so inform the audience. Often during the tests they felt the muscles of my arms, and found them soft and pliant.

At this time I had only one other test to try the "Power." This was what was known everywhere as the "Umbrella Test." The umbrella is opened and a man grasps the handle, with one hand high up and the other lower down towards the end of the handle. I place one of my hands between his, the open palm along the staff. The person is required to hold the umbrella and himself steady. This always proved a very amusing and exciting test.

It was so on this my first public occasion. After having my hand on it a moment, it began to gyrate. It took on more life and a different species of life from the chair or the cane. It has the quick, darting, buoyant life of some mighty enraged bird scurrying and darting about in the air, while the chair, the cane, etc., exhibit that of a strong beast struggling on its feet. A balloon let loose could not exhibit more energy than this umbrella. An eagle battling for its young could not be quicker nor fiercer in its ferocity. The umbrella darted its projecting ribs at every body around, just like an eagle would its bill when rushing upon its enemy. It flopped its cover as a vulture does its wings. It seemed to get inflated with a species of restless gas that knew nothing but perpetual motion, and tried always to get away from the victim under its folds. It pulled the man hither and thither, and it required all of his attention to keep his feet upon the floor and his head off of it. In the meantime the vicious darting of the ribs had cleared the stage of the dignified committee, after several of them had been jobbed unceremoniously, and had come near losing their eyes. All at once the collapse came. The umbrella turned inside out, as though a cyclone had struck it, and the man went headforemost upon the floor.

Then different phases of these same tests were tried. The audience crowded up, each one wanting a taste of what they considered the " Supernatural Force." And one by one they got it. Some of them were hurled off of the stage by the strange power, and caught by the audience below. Many of them had their garments torn more or less, or bursted from their bodies. All who tried it were shocked, exhausted and overcome by the "Force."

I did not know, I could not realize, the extent of the excitement. So far as I ever knew, there was not a skeptic in the house. Not one who tried it was. From this night my confidence in my " Power " and myself never wavered or weakened.

Several newspaper men from Rome, Cartersville, Atlanta, and other points in Georgia were there that night. The next day I found myself famous all over my native State, and requests coming in for me to exhibit elsewhere.

I had crossed the Rubicon—what was I to do next?

CHAPTER V.

ON THE STAGE IN GEORGIA.

Lulu Hurst Becomes the " Georgia Wonder"—The Weird " Table Rapping Test."—Some Interesting Incidents— The Conquest of Modern Rome—An Exciting Scene at Rome—Some of the Romans who Danced to the Music of the "Power."

I think it is my duty to myself and to my readers to state just here that at this time I had not discovered the real nature and source of my power, nor the laws governing it. I will explain in Part II. when and how the mystery began to be solved by me. It was a long time after this. • What astonished me more than the mysterious force itself was the wonderful effect it had upon the people. This was indeed a revelation to me in human nature or in psychology, which was startling, and perhaps as wonderful to me as my power was to them. As we progress with this narrative, I will cite many remarkable incidents in illustration of this imbecility, I will term it, of human reason. This thought impresses me at the time of writing this book, in my maturer years, since having solved the mystery of the Power, with much more force than it did then. The reader may think it strange at the outset of my stage career, that I could not give a rational explanation of this apparently "Supernatural Power," but I could not, nor could the most learned men on the continent, who had every opportunity to test it and explain it. Such savants were acquainted with all the known laws of physics, mechanics and psychology. I, the "Child Wonder," was acquainted with none of them. But I did not get up superstitious ideas on the subject. A great many people would say to me: "You are a 'Spirit Medium' of a high order. A Spirit Band does these wonderful things through you." To me this appeared as silly nonsense and rank superstition. One of my tests, which I have not yet referred to, was this: I would place my hands on a table, and in a few minutes knocks or "raps," as they are called, would begin *in* and *on the wood of the table.* They would come at different points on and in the wood—some slight and others very loud. These raps would answer questions and do many remarkable things; they told people's ages, the time of day, incidents about people's lives and family history, and seemed to foretell events. I did not introduce this test on the stage for the reasons I will give at the proper time and place. But a great many people tested it privately, and were mystified over it. It seemed to produce a superstitious awe in their minds. But I did not look upon it as a so-called occult phenomenon, as I will explain later. Yet think of the thousands of people who are duped by this phenomenon and made the victims of the grossest superstition. In the proper place a full account will be given of how and why these "raps" occur. I know the explanation will set at rest the minds and consciences of vast numbers of people.   But, as I said before, during the whole time I was on the stage I could not explain rationally any of these tests and phenomena.   My parents, who watched every indication of the " Power " in me from the beginning, were in absolute darkness about it.

Mr. Paul M. Atkinson, my manager while I was on the stage (now my husband), was at as much a loss to account for it as any one in the audience.   They regarded the " Power " as some occult phenomenon, but took no stock in the " Spiritualistic theory."   I make these remarks here in the beginning to show that the " Force " was an unknown quantity to all of us.

*   *   *   *   *   *

Well, after my very successful experience in Cedartown, we had to make up our minds quickly as to our future course.   We were soon besieged on every hand with inquiries, letters, telegrams, requests, persuasions, etc., etc. Rome, Chattanooga, Atlanta, and other cities and towns called for an exhibition by the " Georgia Wonder," as I was then called.

If I remember correctly, a committee came down from Rome headed by Mr. Ponder, editor of the Rome *Daily Bulletin*, urgently begging us to give an exhibition there at once.   We deliberated over it and discussed it.   We felt ourselves in a peculiarly embarrassing position.   The manifestation of the Power had aroused the public curiosity to a white heat, and the public demanded that it be satisfied.   I did not relish the notoriety.   My father's " Baptist deacon " ideas were greatly shocked, and his conscience had to become reconciled to the propriety of the " deacon's daughter " going on the stage.   But, to cut matters short, we finally decided to yield to these urgent requests. The Rome committee came, saw, and conquered. To Rome we went.

Here we met with an enthusiastic audience. The day of the entertainment a number of newspaper men, citizens, and physicians were invited to a private exhibition. They were amazed at what they saw, and spread the news of the " Wonder " over the city. So far as I can now remember there were but few skeptics in Rome that I heard of. One of them was Dr. G. W. Holmes, one of the most eminent physicians in the South, and for a number of years a partner of the world-renowned Dr. Robert Battey. Dr. Holmes did not believe there was anything abnormal or occult in my power, and, like Dr. Hammond of New York, would not come to test it. He said : " Nature would not contradict her laws nor defy the faculty of reason she had placed in man to create any number of 'Georgia Wonders.'" On the other hand, the distinguished Dr. J. B. S. Holmes (a nephew of Dr. G. W. Holmes), who has established in Atlanta, Ga., the finest sanitorium in the South (the Halcyon), was a firm believer in the Wonder. His remark to my father, after he had thoroughly tested the Power, was: "She is the Wonder of the century, an anomaly surpassing my understanding. My advice to you is to make the most of it while it lasts, for it may cease as suddenly as it came."

The other skeptic, whose individuality is impressed very visibly on my memory, is one whose name I will not give through deference to him, and on account of the unpleasant occurrence which I will relate. From what I have since learned about him, I know him to be a big-hearted, kind, genial gentlemen, and highly thought of by all who know him. But he is an impulsive man, and it was doubtless on the impulse of the moment that he brought about the unpleasant incident connected with my Rome exhibition. He was one of the kind of skeptics who believed in making the investigation, and in demonstrating the doubt within him. So he came to my exhibition. In observing the manner of my tests in exhibiting the "Power," my father had seen that there was great danger to myself, if the objects experimented with, such as chairs, canes, billiard cues, umbrellas, etc., were not firmly held by the experimenter. He was very much afraid of the "Power" any way, and was in mortal dread that it would hurt me. He had several times seen me come near being injured by these objects being held loosely and carelessly, and allowed to fly from the person, or out of the grasp of the holder. So, my or his request to every one, if they tried the test was, to protect me by keeping firm hold of the object. This request was made of this gentleman, for he had come on the stage to try the "Power."

But he would not comply with the request after the experiment began, saying that he would demonstrate it in his own way. The consequence was that when he took hold of the chair, instead of holding it firmly, he, to all appearances, purposely let it fly off from him, and the chair flirted over and struck me in the face. This no sooner occurred, than on the impulse of the moment, my father (who was a quick, impulsive man himself) grabbed up a chair and struck the gentleman a severe blow. The excitement caused by this was very great indeed. The audience came near stampeding. Nothing ever happened during my stage life which we all regretted more than this. My father especially was deeply sorry for it, and wrote the gentleman afterwards expressing his regrets and asking his forgiveness.

*   *   *   *   *   *

I would not have referred to this, the only unfortunate occurrence of the kind during my stage career, were it not that I desire to use the incident as an object-lesson, to show exactly how my father viewed the "Power," and how sincere he was in his ideas about it.

Another thing occurred in Rome which was of vast importance to us. Our fame had been heralded from Cedartown with such a blow of trumpets, that it had reached the big brain of the great Henry Grady, of the *Atlanta Constitution*. Mr. Grady at once sent Mr. Josiah Carter, that brilliant journalist, who is now the able managing editor of the *Atlanta Journal*, to Cedartown, to investigate and report these wild rumors, which were coming to him from Polk county in reference to the "Wonderful Girl." When Mr. Carter arrived at Cedartown, he learned that I had gone to Rome to give an exhibition there. He followed us to Rome, and there in the parlors of the hotel he met the object of his search. I gave him a short, private exhibition, and he was fully convinced of the marvelous power. He was so deeply impressed both *on body* and *in mind*, that he prepared, as only his glowing pen could do, a two-columned article for the *Constitution*. To give his article more force, he returned, after seeing me in Rome, to my home in quaint Cedar Valley, and poetically depicted the surroundings of my childhood residence, and made a sketch of our house showing the old ante-bellum style of architecture with the broad veranda and white-fluted columns in front, sitting well back in a beautiful grove. His splendid article appeared in the *Constitution* over the author's signature, and being the first extended leading article about me in one of the nation's greatest papers, it gave an impetus to my growing fame that was far-reaching in its results to me.

*　　*　　*　　*　　*　　*

The Rome *Daily Bulletin* in an exhaustive article descriptive of the performance given in Rome, says: "The Nevin Opera House was crowded last night to see the exhibition of the wonderful power of Lulu Hurst. Many of our leading citizens were on the stage pitting their muscular force against the mysterious powers of the fair young "Wonder" of Cedar Valley. Among a great number who took part in the tests were: Col. D. S. Printup, Mayor King, Dr. Bunting, Mr. C. M. Harper, Dr. Tigner, Mr. John Bowie and Mr. R. H. West. A more thoroughly handled crowd of men has not been seen in many a day. * * * * The power was invincible and showed them no consideration. Chairs, canes and umbrellas seemed like infuriated demons of energy, and dragged and hurled these dignified Romans about, as though they had been mere toys, puppets and playthings. * * * * It was amusing to see with what energy Col. Harper cut the pigeon-wing, and with what grace the portly Dr. Tigner knocked the back-step, and with what swiftness Mayor King could swing corners. * * * * The house was hilarious and wildly enthusiastic. It was fun and mystery mixed in wild confusion."

CHAPTER VI.

THE ASSAULT ON ATLANTA.

Hon. Hoke Smith a Skeptic Concerning the Power—Hon. Henry W. Grady a Convert—A Strange Coincidence in My Life Connected with Mr. Grady—A Sad and Tragic Scene in the Atlanta Opera House—The Conversion of Col. Tomlinson Fort in Chattanooga—Mr. George Ochs of the Chattanooga Times Remains a Hardened Unbeliever— The Quandary of the Learned Faculty of Mercer University.

From Rome we went to Atlanta for two exhibitions at DeGive's Opera House. My fame had preceded me and the result was crowded houses. The same tests of the "Power" were used here as before, and two new tests were added. I will describe these. A gentleman was requested to sit in a strong chair, grasp the seat on either side, and hold the chair firmly, and tilt it so as to throw all his weight on its rear legs. I then placed my open palms on the upper part of the two upright posts of the back, and, without grasping the chair in the least, lifted it six inches from the floor. I then had a man weighing over two hundred pounds sit in the chair in the same manner, and had another heavy man sit in his lap, and still another occupant on the shoulder of the second man. The aggregate weight of the

Digitized by Google

three would amount to five hundred pounds, or over. I then placed the palm of my hands upon the posts of the chair in the same way as before, and lifted the combined weight six inches from the floor. Of course such a test as this created unbounded enthusiasm.

My other new test was to have one or two or more men attempt to press a billiard cue to the floor while my open palm was against it, the cue being held in an upright position. This test was as successful as the others. None could push the cue across my palm to the floor. I say it without boasting, I carried the vast Atlanta audience as by storm. Among the thousand or more, who saw me at each performance, there were but three skeptics that I ever heard of. One of these was the Hon. Hoke Smith, who was at that time one of the most successful lawyers in the State, and whose name has since become connected with the history of the Executive Department of our National Government. He was on the stage during one of the performances, and after watching the tests closely, stated to the audience that he believed he could demonstrate the force underlying these manifestations of Power. But as was usually the case with me everywhere, the audience was so enthused and in sympathy with the "Power," that Mr. Smith soon found it was more difficult to make his explanation to an Atlanta audience than it was to win a great railroad case, or manage a great afternoon *Journal.*

The other two skeptics were Col. Burton Smith, now one of the leading railroad lawyers of the State and Mr. Smith Clayton, one of our most versatile Southern journalists. Our entertainment was a big financial success as well as otherwise, and the "Georgia Wonder" was the chief topic

of discussion on the streets of Atlanta the next day.   The
Atlanta papers gave our exhibition very prominent and
flattering notices.   On this day Mr. Henry Grady called to
see me, and requested that we accompany him to his office,
which we did.   And there, in company with my father and
mother, and other friends, he tested the "Power" in every
conceivable way, and was fully convinced that it was beyond his comprehension, and so affirmed.   From that day
until I left the stage he was my friend, steadfast and true,
as was his nature, and his great paper was my staunch sup-
porter and champion.   He and the *Constitution* followed
me all during my strange stage career with great interest.
He wrote and published many pleasant things about me. This
of course endeared him to me ever afterwards.   This brings
me to relate a strange coincidence—on the same day that
this Noble Life went out my baby boy was born, and, my
husband also being an ardent admirer of this great man,
we called our baby "Grady."

I will give a few quotations from the very full account
given in the Atlanta *Journal* of one of our exhibitions, in
which is described a very sad and somewhat tragic occurrence.   I will not give the estimable young lady's name
out of deference to her and her family, who are among the
best people of the State.   This occurrence but faintly
illustrates to what extent the public excitement was wrought
up by my performances.

The article is headed:

"LULU HURST LAST NIGHT."

*"A Sad and Exciting Scene in the Opera House"—"A
Lady's Nervous Excitement over Miss Hurst's Wonderful
Performance Creates a Sensation."*

"An immense audience assembled at the Opera House last night to greet Miss Lulu Hurst's second appearnace in Atlanta. Her performances grow more wonderful and marvelous all the time.   *   *   *   *   *   *

"The following gentlemen, and others upon invitation from Mr. Atkinson, the manager, came upon the stage to take part in the experiments: Mr. Fulton Colville, Dr. Catching, Officer Reed, Dr. Delbridge, Mr. R. B. Evans, Mr. J. R. Scott, Mr. H. S. Smith, Mr. Fairbanks, Mr. H. H. Tucker, Jr., Mr. James Moser, and others.

"Among others who went upon the stage was a tall, savage-looking individual with piercing eyes and large moustache. He wore a blue flannel shirt and an overcoat with extra long tail. He wore his breeches in his boots, and there was an air of comicality in his appearance which provoked the audience to laughter and hearty cheering. An hundred voices in the gallery cried out, 'Boots! boots! boots!' and the queer looking customer turned to the audience, and waving his left hand made a deep bow. He then took his seat and was a quiet and interested spectator. The man's name was W. W. Webster, a professional horse trainer from Kentucky.

" The tests began.

" Mr. Fulton Colville engaged Miss Hurst in the first test. He took an ordinary chair in his arms, and by pressing it firmly against his breast, endeavored to hold it still. Miss Hust touched it gently and the chair commenced moving about. Mr. Colville was compelled to move around over the stage. He could not stand still. He danced a furious quick-step all over the stage, and the audience roared. He finally gave up the contest, and Mr. Evans, the largest man on the stage, tried to hold the chair, but he could not do so, though the audience shouted to him to 'Hold it, hold it; stand still and hold it.' The same test was tried by Mr. H. S. Smith, and he was no more successful in his attempt than the others had been. There was then the cry of 'Boots! boots! boots!' and the curious Kentuckian arose and took the chair in his grasp. He was more stately and dignified in appearance, and the many in the audience, who were on the tiptoe of expectation that a flood of fun would follow, were somewhat abashed by the sober demeanor and gentlemanly bearing of 'Boots.' He grasped the chair firmly. He held it still for just a moment. Then it moved a little, it jerked to one side and bobbed up, and then bore downward, but 'Boots' held it with all his might. It arose and fell and then surged like a wild vulture, dragging 'Boots' tumultuously over the stage. He then turned to the audience and said: 'Gentlemen and ladies, or ladies and gentlemen, as I should have said [applause], I came up here for your merriment. I profess to know something about this power. I know what it is, and I tell you there is not a man on earth who can hold that chair.'

"Dr. Catching and Officer Reed next tried the test, and their fate was the common fate of all. They were defeated and vanquished as the others had been. At this point the excitement on the stage and in the audience had reached the highest tension, and in the midst of it a scene as sad and exciting as any that ever transpired in Atlanta took place.

"Suddenly, a young lady in the audience arose and exclaimed in a wild and excited manner:

" ' Woman shall not rule the world; that is man's province, and woman shall not rule the world ! '

" For a time the audience was unable to comprehend the meaning of the singular demonstration, and there was applause in many portions of the house. The lady, who had given utterance to these strange words, was Miss ——, a sister of Rev. ——, of this city, and the excitement in consequence of the wonderful performance had completely unstrung her nerves, and for the time she was transformed and thoroughly incensed against Miss Hurst for having overpowered a dozen strong and powerful men.

" ' Woman shall not rule the world,' said she. ' Let me get to her,' and she attempted to gain the middle aisle leading to the stage. ' Sit down, my sister. Oh, my sister, please be quiet and take your seat,' said a gentleman. ' I will not sit down,' said she ; ' I will go to Lulu Hurst. A woman shall not prevail.'

" By this time she had succeeded in getting into the aisle, and, pulling away from her friend, went hurriedly in the direction of the stage. The wildest excitement prevailed, and many in the audience, who did not comprehend the . situation, continued to cheer. Rev. —— tried to quiet her, but he could not do so, and then by a wave of his hand he quieted the audience and said : ' Ladies and gentlemen, this is my sister. Please be patient and I will endeavor to quiet her as soon as possible.'

" By this time she had reached the foot of the stage, and endeavored to enter the door leading from the parquet to the rear of the stage, but the door was closed and she was prevented from doing so. She felt that she was able to overcome Miss Hurst, and it was her idea to go upon the stage and engage her in the test. No one could do anything with her, and some of her friends, thinking it best to allow her to go upon the stage, had the door opened for that purpose; but those nearest thought differently and prevented her from going. Then, tearing away from those around her, she stood up in a chair and made an effort to climb over the footlights to the stage, but she was prevented also from doing this. Some one on the stage cried out, 'Lulu Hurst has been taken away.' This had a good effect and she became more quiet. Step by step, slowly, and by the kindest coaxing, she was led from the opera house. Dr. Love was present and gave her some brandy, which seemed to quiet her very much. She was placed in a carriage and driven to her home. As she left the hall in charge of friends, her brother, whose heart was full of grief and deep emotion, ascended the orchestral platform in front of the stage and addressed the audience.

"Mr. Atkinson, who had kept his wits about him all the time, led Miss Hurst off the stage when the excitement began, and she did not appear again until Miss —— had left the hall. It was feared by many that if the young lady had gained the stage Miss Hurst would have been injured in some way.

"When Mr. —— and his sister had gone, Mr. Atkinson said:

"'I feel fully assured, ladies and gentlemen, that I speak the sentiment of every person in this house when I say that the gentleman and his unfortunate sister have the heartfelt sympathy of this entire audience. It is natural for us to sympathize with each other in misfortune, and we regret exceedingly that this distressing circumstance has occurred. We sincerely hope the lady may soon recover her nerves and be herself again.'

" The audience quieted down and the entertainment was renewed.

" Miss —— is a most estimable young lady and is highly cultured. She possesses a rare musical talent, and her pleasant manner and kind and affectionate disposition have endeared her to a large circle of friends. She is resting quietly to-day, and, we are glad to say, is quite herself again.

" No man was ever in a more trying position than that in which Mr. —— found himself placed last night, and no man could have assumed a more dignified and manly demeanor than that which characterized his speech and action in the terrible hour. He touched the very soul of the audience, when in his last extremity he exclaimed, ' She is my sister, friends, and I cannot lay violent hands upon her. It will all soon be right.'

" There was not a man or woman in the vast audience whose heart did not go out to him in his distress, and the pathetic scene, in its tender appeal to the diviner emotions of the soul, filled many eyes with tears. He had the heartfelt sympathy of the great audience." * * * * * *

Here follows a description of various other tests given of the " Power," and the article concludes: " All the gentlemen on the stage gave a public expression of opinion concerning the ' Wonderful Power,' the unanimous verdict being that the Power was one which could not be understood."

From Atlanta we went to Chattanooga, where our success was all that we could desire. In Chattanooga we met

two skeptics.   One of these was Mr. George Ochs, the
editor of the *Chattanooga Times*, the ablest journal in the
State.   Mr. Ochs is at present the mayor of the city, and
one of the most efficient Chattanooga has ever had.

The other skeptic was Col. Tomlinson Fort.   He is one
of the leading lawyers of Tennessee, a man of very positive convictions, and a deep thinker, close observer and
reasoner, possessing a strong judicial mind of keen acumen
and analytical power.   He is also one of the best informed
men in the South.   He was very skeptical of the " Power"
until he saw the different tests, whereupon he became,
like many other skeptics when they investigated it, a
firm and enthusiastic believer.   He made a splendid
speech to the audience, and among other things said that
until that moment he had never believed anything which
could not be accounted for along the line of reason.
" But," said he, " there is no sense nor reason in this
thing, and yet I am obliged to believe it because here it is
taking place right before my eyes."

But Mayor George Ochs, like Hon. Hoke Smith, was
never convinced, so far as I could ascertain.

Leaving Chattanooga, we resumed our trip through
Georgia, giving entertainments at all the principal towns
and cities.

In Macon, Georgia, we gave a private exhibition before
the faculty of Mercer University, which was composed of
the following eminent gentlemen, some of whom have
national reputations :

Professor J. E. Willet, the learned physicist and author
of a standard work on " Insect Life," a close observer and
trained investigator.   He recently died, at a ripe age,

in Atlanta, Georgia, and his loss is mourned throughout
the State.   Dr. A. J. Battle, President of the University
and a Baptist minister of deep learning.   He is the author
of that scholarly volume, "Battle on the Human Will,"
and various treatises on doctrinal and abstruse subjects.
He is withal a magnificent gentleman, with all the polish
and erudition and suavity of manner of a scholar of the
"Old Southern School."

Dr. J. J. Brantley, known as the greatest master of
pure English style and diction in the South, and a learned
rhetorician and logician.

Professor Sanford, the distinguished author of Sanford's
series of arithmetics, which have been adopted as text-books
in the schools and colleges all over the country.

Professor Steed, a ripe scholar and a most proficient in-
structor in Latin and Greek ; and Dr. Rials, the well-known
divine, who so ably fills the Chair of Theology.

This important investigation of the "Power" by this
learned faculty was extensively written about in the State
papers.   I quote the following account from a long article
published at the time in the Augusta *Chronicle*.   The article goes into a great many details, and after pronouncing
me "The Greatest Wonder of the Nineteenth Century,"
says :

"Professor Battle brought in a new umbrella. Miss Hurst
then took the umbrella, and, as she touched it, the article flew
about the room, and Professor Battle was forced to release
his hold.   Miss Hurst then picked up the umbrella and it
immediately flew to pieces. She then took a large stick,
Professor Battle, Dr. Brantley, and others endeavoring
to hold it; both were necessitated to jump about the

room like jumping-jacks. Professor Willet took hold
of the stick, but was immediately forced to let loose
his hold. Miss Hurst invited all in the room to
hold the stick; she could, by her touch, force them
all to dance around. She then took a chair, which several
of the gentlemen in the room endeavored to hold, but without success.

"Miss Hurst, by her touch, forced them around the room
and against the wall. She then asked two or three of the
faculty to put the chair on the floor with all their strength
and pressure. The simple touch of her hand prevented its
reaching the floor. This test astonished the professors,
creating untold surprise at her power, which in the words of
Professor Battle, 'Baffles explanation and defies definition.'

"Miss Hurst then requested any of the Faculty to suggest
any experiments. Several questions were put and experiments tried, which only tended to add to the wonder of
these scientific men. Professor Willet, being asked whether
he thought Miss Hurst's power magnetic, electric, or spirit-
itualistic, answered: 'I have studied the subject with
much thought. It is wonderful, yes marvelous, almost, I
should say, miraculous; but I am more astonished than ever
after my investigation.'

"After an hour and a half in wonderland, Miss Hurst
bade the faculty of Mercer University good-bye, leaving
these wise men wondering over this mysterious Georgia
girl.

"That her performance was a success was indorsed by
all the faculty; that her force was not muscular was quite
evident, as there was no exertion or exhaustion on her part,
while the several strong men, who grasped and tugged at

the objects she touched, were physically outdone, and, under such circumstances, to attribute it to muscular power,
would make the effortless display of a timid girl inexplicable and greater than the combined strength of three men,
either of whom could overpower her in a personal encounter.
So the question as to whether her powers are magnetic,
electric, or spiritualistic is as far from settled as ever. It is
suggested that your great scientist, Dr. Raines, endeavor to
solve this wonderful mystery when Miss Hurst reaches
Augusta."

CHAPTER VII.

LIVELY TIMES IN MODERN ATHENS, GEORGIA'S "CLASSIC CITY."

A Pen Picture by the Inimitable Lary Gantt—Professor H. C. White, of the State University, a Skeptic—A Meeting which Shaped my Destiny for Life—The Mystified Faculty of the Augusta Medical College—A Panic in the Augusta Opera House Quelled—A Strange Séance with the Late Hon. Thomas Gibson.

The occasion I write about was our second visit to Athens, Georgia's Classic City, a city of wealth and refinement, and the seat of the State University and the Famous Lucy Cobb Female College, and other noted institutions of learning.

We gave a private exhibition of the "Power" there, which was attended by many learned men. They made a great number of tests. Out of that body I never learned of but one witness who went away skeptical as to the occult nature of the "Power." This was the distinguished Professor H. C. White, professor of physics and chemistry in the State University.

In all descriptions of our entertainments in papers all over the continent, I have seldom read anything so rich, rare, and racy as Mr. Lary Gantt's article in the Athens *Banner* descriptive of my exhibition there.

It illustrates the rare gifts of this journalist even in dealing with as difficult and mysterious a subject as the "Georgia Wonder." Lary Gantt is inimitable. As a writer and journalist he is *sui generis.* He is a mixture of Henry Grady and Bill Nye. The rich stye of the article is my excuse for quoting so largely from it.

The article is headed:

"THE ELECTRIC MAID.

"Athens Turns out en Masse to Greet Lulu Hurst on Her Return from a Triumphant Tour Over the Union—The Opera House Packed from Pit to Dome—Miss Lulu's Powers Increased, and Her Exhibitions still More Wonderful—Interview with the Party and their Past and Future Movements.

The first part of the article is a description of myself and of our tour over the continent, and of our great success on the stage and financially. Then follows the description of our Athens performance :

"At 8 o'clock the curtain arose on the largest and most refined audience we have ever seen assembled in our opera-house. Every seat was taken, and the aisles packed with gentlemen standing. We noticed that not only the business walks of life, but even the Bar, the College, and the Pulpit had contributed their quota towards tendering Miss Lulu a hearty welcome to Athens. * * * * * *

"And another thing impressed us, the marked courtesy and respect with which the entertainment was treated throughout the evening. You heard none of the rude applause and jests generally made on such occasions, but the best order and the most intense interest was displayed. This little incident proves that our people, not only look with just pride upon Miss Lulu, but they feel for her a most profound respect, knowing her to be a lady of whom our State may well feel vain.

"Mr. Atkinson, in a few well-chosen words, in which he spoke of the numerous tests of Miss Hurst's mysterious power, made by the most learned scientists in Washington City and elsewhere, and stating that they were at a loss to account for it, introduced Mrs. Hurst and Miss Lulu. These ladies acknowledged the applause which greeted their names by a polite bow. Invitations were then extended any gentlemen in the audience to come upon the stage and test Miss Lulu's powers, and about a dozen promptly stepped forward.

"The Electric Maid first asked the editor of this paper to try his muscle, but he declined on the plea that a burnt child dreads fire; our wounds received twelve months ago just beginning to heal well. But when she turned those magnetic eyes upon us full of some wonderful drawing power, we could resist no longer, and with the resignation of a martyr pranced to the front. Miss Lulu whispered to us that she had her powers under better control than at first, and would handle us tenderly and with care. We grasped the chair, closed our eyes, braced our muscles, and sent up a prayer for safety.

"Miss Lulu gently rested one of her soft hands upon a round, and in about two seconds' time we felt ourself giving away all over, and an uncontrollable desire to travel. Whether we held on to the chair, or the chair held on to us, will be an unsolved mystery to our dying day. Anyhow we were as firmly joined together as a pair of Siamese twins, and that inanimate piece of wood and white-oak splits began to wheel us around the stage in a regular old-fashioned Virginia breakdown. It swung corners with us, promenaded all, backed to places, and, in fact, did everything except change partners, a termination we so earnestly longed for. The chair tried to throw us over the footlights, rammed us between the scenes, and at last was making way with us for a side window, when Mr. Atkinson whispered in our ear not to let the chair loose. Let it loose! Why we would have given half of our wealth to have been able to let it loose. That chair clung to us closer than a brother, and had it been fastened to our back instead of pinned on our breast, like a hotel clerk's diamond, we would have felt like a modern edition of Sinbad the Sailor, when the old man of the sea used him for a riding-horse. At last Miss Lulu seemed to take pity on us, and removing her hands the spell was broken. * * * * * *

"Bode, the baker, then came to the bat, with a look that plainly said, 'I'd like to see you kneed me like you did that insignificant ink-slinger.' At a single glance Miss Lulu took in Bode from that patch of flour on his nose to the mud on his boots. He seized the chair and took his position with a confidence that would have even made the Rock of Gibraltar ashamed of itself. But a change soon came over the spirit of his dreams. Bode suddenly took a notion that he wanted to 'exodust' to Kansas or some other distant clime, and began a backward retreat that would have done no discredit to a healthy land-crab. But Miss Lulu was determined to be revenged on her victim

for that confident air, and she took him on a regular old
tare. She used Bode as she would a shuck mop, to wipe
up the floor. At one time he thought he was going
through the ceiling, and when the poor man seemed to be
in the expiring agonies of misery, he was quietly seated on
top of a gas jet, when he retired to a chair with the seat of
his pants ablaze. Mr. Bode's nerves were not soothed by
a friend informing him that the footlights were intended
for illuminating purposes, and not seats to sit upon. But
he was not satisfied—he said Miss Lulu had a young cyclone hid somewhere about her, and anybody could throw
a fellow around with such a force. * * * * * *

"The Electric Maid then took the other volunteers in
hand one by one, and it is needless to add that leaf by leaf
the roses fell. It mattered not whether she tackled a Tom
Thumb or a Goliath, the result was the same. Soon the
stage was filled with red-faced, perspiring, wind-broken
humanity, while the fragile maid of Cedar Valley was as
tranquil as a spring morning, and ordered the deck cleared
for fresh action. More gallant knights came forward, or
more properly speaking, lambs to the slaughter. She went
through the billiard cue, the umbrella and the chair
tests with the most wonderful success, and floored a dozen
men as easily as one. A whole pyramid of giants tried to
force a chair to the floor against the posts of which the
fair young girl's hand slightly rested, but they had as well
try to turn over Stone Mountain. She also placed two
heavy men in a chair and raised it clear off the floor by the
gentle pressure of her hand. We watched her face and
every muscle, and will assert that not a particle of force
was used. But a new and most wonderful test of Miss

Lulu's mysterious power was when she stood on one foot and the greatest exertions of stout men pushing against a billiard cue she held in her hands could not throw her off-ballance. This test should certainly convince the most skeptical that there is neither trick nor exertion used in giving these wonderful performances. At the conclusion of the entertainment, if there was a single doubter among the large audience, he did not make himself known. Two of the stoutest men in our city came forward with the fixed determination to force the end of a billiard cue that lay flat against her palm, to the floor, but not only they made a failure, but as many men as could find hand-hold failed to accomplish it."

Long will we cherish the memory of the genial, refined, hospitable people of the beautiful Classic City, but none more than the big-hearted genius, Lary Gantt.

To me the most important incident of my stage career, and one that shaped my destiny for life, occurred some time before this at the beautiful and hospitable little city of Madison, Ga., which is now my home. Here I met many pleasant acquaintances, and among them a young gentleman, Mr. Paul M. Atkinson, who soon thereafter became my manager. He proved himself in every way thoroughly fitted to do this work, and was untiring in his efforts to make my entertainments successful everywhere. His position was a trying and arduous one, and one that required much tact and ability to successfully handle. But he measured up to all of the requirements so well, and made my tours so eminently successful and pleasant, that in after years, in order to reward him and give myself a very great pleasure in the bargain, I did not do a thing but—marry him.

At Augusta, Georgia, we gave a private entertainment at the State Medical College before the faculty and students, and I think I can safely say that, while there were many doubting Thomases before the exhibition, yet after all the tests they proposed were gone through with, they were all firm believers. They took my temperature immediately after the performance of one marvellous feat after another, and could see no perceptible change. They placed their hands under mine and felt no appreciable pressure. Dr. Raines, the president of the College at that time, and one of the foremost of the older school of physicians in the South, and an able scientist, was intensely interested in all of the phenomena of the "Power," and especially so in the "table rapping test." After hearing these strange sounds emitted out of the wood of the table, he secured a little bell and tied it under the table for the purpose of letting the "Unknown Force" ring the bell; but he was disappointed in getting any such a manifestation as this. He was ready to expect almost any sort of phenomena to occur. I think, as a rule, physicians were the most skeptical before they had tried the tests, but afterwards they were my most earnest converts.

While giving a performance in the opera-house in Augusta before a large audience, an incident occurred which came near proving a calamity. It also illustrates several phases of human nature, the conclusions from which the reader may draw for himself. The exhibition throughout had been very successful, and intensely exciting. One marvelous test after another of the "Power" had set the audience wild. In the height of the excitement a storm came up, and suddenly a great gust of wind blew off some of the tin roof which came down with a crash. Well, the audience was just ripe for any thing, no matter how wonderful, and many of them actually thought the "Power" was tearing the house down; many made a break for the door, and it took quick action and cool heads to quell the panic. The next day there was great wonderment and enthusiasm throughout the city.

When in Augusta we became acquainted with that most pleasant and genial gentleman, Thomas Gibson, then of the *Evening News*, whose sad death in a far off country, where he represented our government, has so recently sent a thrill of bereavement to the hearts of his multitude of friends in Georgia. He came to call on us at the Globe Hotel, and while there asked that we try with him the weird table rapping test. It was very successful. The mysterious raps in and on the wood of the table came in quick and loud thuds and knocks. They told him many things about himself and family which he considered very wonderful. I remember there was an important murder trial going on in the city. The case had been argued by Judge H. D. D. Twiggs on one side, and Hon. J. C. C. Black on the other. The jury was out and the public anxiously awaiting their verdict. Mr. Gibson wanted an acquittal, and the raps on the table gave it to him. He was so excited over it that he grabbed his hat and hurried to the court-house. My recollection now is the acquittal came. Noble, genial "Judge" Gibson, as he was called—little did we then dream of the sad, tragic end that was destined to be his lot. He was one of Nature's noblemen.

CHAPTER VIII.

DID THE POWER MOVE THE STALLED ENGINE AND TRAIN OF CARS? TAKING THE ELASTICITY OUT OF STEEL.

The Big-hearted Matt O'Brien Suffers from the Butt End of his own Joke—"Laying on of Hands"—Strange Vagaries in the Minds of Some People— Did they Believe the "Power" to be Unlimited?

The above caption to this chapter was suggested to my mind by actual occurrences, which I will narrate just as they took place.

In our travels all over the continent from place to place, we were remarkably fortunate in always making our connections and being on time for our appointments. On our entire trip we never missed a train or left a piece of our baggage. We traveled more than twenty thousand miles without an accident, and only on a few occasions was our train delayed.

I remember once we were coming from Americus to Macon, Georgia, and were delayed by a freight-train which, being overloaded, and the engine partly disabled, had struck a steep grade and could not get over it. After some delay and annoyance our engine went to the rescue. Unfortunately about this time the freight engine became so disabled as to be almost useless, and it seemed that our engine was unable to do the work unaided. The situation was growing very serious. It was known among the passengers that I was on the train, so some one informed the conductor that "Miss Lulu Hurst was aboard, and that they believed *she could move the train.*" As I learned afterwards the conductor had seen one of my performances and had unlimited faith in the "Power." Imagine my surprise when he came back and asked me to help him out of his trouble. Well, it occurred to me that I had nothing to lose and everything to gain should my power prove of help to him in his great emergency, and I told him that I did not know whether I could do him any good or not, but if I could render him any assistance I would gladly do so. So he asked me to come to the engine with him. By this time all the passengers were cognizant of what was going on, and they became deeply interested. The engineer and I, with some of the other passengers, left the coach and went to the engine. The engineer assisted me to a position by his side in the cab of the mighty machine, which stood puffing a tired, slow, solemn whiff! whiff! I took my position and told him to put on a full head of steam and when he was ready to let me know, and then open the throttle, and I would try to help him over the grade. He did as I directed, and then told me he was ready; I put my hands on the engine and it started. And lo! up the grade it went, on and up to the top without stopping. The passengers had kept apace with us as best they could, and when they saw the successful pull, such a yell arose as is seldom heard from the throats of enthusiastic people. What their views

were at that moment of the "Power" and what was the
limit of their faith in it, I will not attempt to say. An
account of this incident appeared in the newspapers and
was written up in modern sensational style.

After one of our regular entertainments in Columbus,
Ga., which went off with the same uproarous enthusiasm
as all others I have described, there was quite a party who
remained after the audience left, with the hope of getting
a private chat with me. These demands for private interviews came regularly after every performance, and it became
necessary to either elude them by the rear door, or brave
the party and in a measure, at least, satisfy their curiosity.

In the party at Columbus were the chief of police and
that splendid, jolly gentleman, Mr. Matt O'Brien, who was
at the head of the Southern Express Company in the
South, and whose brother, Colonel O'Brien, is now superintendent of this great company. They were both much
interested in my power, and the chief was anxious to test
it. He carried a small, though strong, black cane, with a
steel rod through the center, which made it very elastic.
He asked me to test the "Power" on this cane and he
would try to hold it. I did so, and in the chief's efforts
to hold it he cut the double shuffle and many other fancy
steps too numerous to mention. After his prolonged tussle
with the "Force," when he came to examine his cane he
found that it had lost its elasticity; it had no more
spring to it than a piece of iron. The next day he carried that cane all over the city wherever he went, and
showed it to hundreds, so I was informed. He said that I
had merely touched it and that my touch had taken every bit
of the temper out of it. The result was that this incident

and the excitement growing out of the chief's version of it, gave me a house that was jammed and packed.

During the performance, Mr. Matt O'Brien, who was always ripe for a joke, brought his wife upon the stage, and stated to the audience that he saw me, by the touch of my hand, take the temper out of the chief's steel cane. "Now," said he to me, "I want you to put your hand on my wife and see if you can't take some of the temper out of her." Well, it was a hit, and brought down the house. But the charming wife was equal to the emergency, and replied:

"Well, Miss Hurst, you may place your hands upon me and have some hope of getting some of the temper, Mr. O'Brien refers to, out of me, but let me give you some advice: dont't touch him with any view of correcting his temper, because I know there is nothing under the sun short of a *stroke of lightning* that can possibly take the temper out of him."

The result was Mr. O'Brien suffered from the butt end of his own joke. He died two years ago, and it pained me much to learn that this genial, bright, big-souled life had gone out. He was a poet of considerable ability, and was one of the most popular men in the South. Everybody knew and loved Matt O'Brien. He was much interested in the "Power," and used to quiz me a great deal about it.

When we were in New York he came to see us and entertained us at his relative's home in Brooklyn.

It was in Columbus, Ga., that I first met Dr. George J. Grimes, a very prominent physician and a man of learning and great ability. He became exceedingly interested in the

"Power," and made many experiments. He wrote elaborate articles to the *Medical Record* about me and the "Force."

*   *   *   *   *   *   *   *   *

Another little queer experience took place while I was in Montgomery, Alabama. Dr. Webb, one of the leading physicians of the city, came on the stage, and was much interested in the "Power." After the entertainment was over, he and his wife and several others remained for a private exhibition. Mrs. Webb was a large, handsome lady of much dignity and culture. Dr. Webb remarked to me that he felt quite sure that I could *cure diseases* by the "laying on of hands." He then told me that his wife was a constant sufferer from neuralgia in one of its worst forms, and asked me if I would not place my hands on her cheek and neck (the seat of her pain) and see what effect it would have. I did as he requested, and in a very short space of time Mrs. Webb's eyes closed and she fell back in a death faint. Some of the party caught her and placed her on a chair. Restoratives were used, and in a short while she opened her eyes, and the first thing she said was: "Oh! I feel so good! I feel just like I had been drinking champagne." Of course this remark broke the anxiety and solemnity of the occasion, and we all laughed heartily. She declared that she was cured.

CHAPTER IX.

A FEW REFLECTIONS BY THE WAY.

---

*Some Humorous and Tragic Scenes—The Affrighted Negro
—Congressman Lester, Hon. F. G. duBignon, and Ex-
Senator Norwood Baffled by the Power—The Mighty
Charleston Gathering—The Enterprising News and
Courier My Friend—Colonel Rion, of Columbia, Bursts
a Blood-vessel Contending with the Power.—A Sad Inci-
dent.*

I think there were two things connected with my performances that accounted for the uniformly crowded houses
we had and the intense excitement of the people while the
exhibitions were in progress. One was the mystery connected with the "Power," the wonder and awe occasioned
by its phenomenal manifestations. People, I have found,
are attracted, charmed and fascinated by the mysterious,
the gruesome, the unreal. Things that are wonderful,
that are beyond their understanding and imagination, appeal to the mind's fancies as nothing else does.

The other intensely attractive feature was this: People
like all exhibitions of feats of strength and great power,
the contending forces of strong men struggling for the

mastery over one another. This is the reason a noted prize-fight between known champions will attract crowds as no other exhibition can. Men will go any distance and pay any sum of money to see it.

Now, when you combine these elements together, as in my case—the element of wonder and the feats of power and championship, you have the qualities that attract the multitude anywhere and everywhere.

The "wonder" and "mystery" in my case were that no one could account for such manifestation of power, bordering on the supernatural, as was associated with me, a mere girl just in her teens.

The exhibition of power was such that it was not like one strong man pitted against one other strong man, but it was any number of strong men contending helplessly against the girl, who proved herself master of them all; and who, so far as they could see, exerted no conscious effort in doing so. They were overpowered in body and bewildered in mind by her, and they knew not how. I have often noticed the utter, absolute astonishment and bewilderment of scientific men, physicians, etc., when they put my "Power" through their tests. They would place their hands under mine and feel no appreciable pressure, and yet with their eyes see a chair, containing five hundred pounds of humanity in it, rise up from the floor. I have had physicians hold the muscles of my arm while undergoing these severe tests, and they would invariably declare to the audience that there was no appreciable muscular contraction. Of course, strange fancies, if not superstitions, arose in their minds at such, to them, abnormal and unnatural display of power. They had more control of their feelings and their expressions about it than the ignorant, but the manifestation of awe and bewilderment could not be entirely suppressed by them. There was only a difference in degree between the scholar, who investigated and found nothing but mystery, and the superstitious, ignorant person, who saw the mystery without the investigation.

This little reflection leads me to say that negroes were, as a general rule, mortally afraid of the "Power." In this connection, a very funny incident happened in Jacksonville, Florida. We were stopping at one of the principal hotels there, and I had given enough entertainments to make myself known to everybody.

My mother and I took our meals in our room. One morning a large, black, moon-eyed-looking negro brought our breakfast and attended us. It amused me beyond expression to notice how he shunned the "Power," and maneuvered to protect himself while he waited on us and handed the dishes. I did several little things to see the effect, and he grew more nervous and "offish," and showed the whites of his eyes to a greater degree. I watched him and his movements to amuse myself, for it was intensely comical, and he evidently took up the idea that I was fixing to work the "Power" on him. Matters went on this way till we finished eating. I remained seated at the table on purpose while the trembling waiter piled up the dishes on his tray to take them out. He did this hurriedly and nervously, and, I saw, very carelessly, in his haste. Finally he raised the tray of dishes upon his hand, in the usual way, and started toward the door, at the same time keeping one eye on me. All at once one of the carelessly piled dishes fell with a crash to the floor, breaking in fragments, and on the same instant the negro gave a bound out of the door, throwing to the floor the tray and its contents and breaking everything to pieces. He never stopped until he reached the kitchen. His tale there was, that "ebery dish in de waiter des hopped up and started toward dat young lady; and 'bout dat time I started fur de kitchen, 'fore she could work her power on dis nigger." The result to me was, that after that, it was impossible to get a negro into that room. I think it was in Savannah, Georgia, where the negroes had a strange superstition about me. I noticed when I went out on the streets that they watched my feet. They never took their eyes off my feet while I was in sight of them. Finally, I asked an old negro what they meant by watching my feet so closely?

"Well, Missy," he replied, "de niggers all say day see de sparks fly outer your feet on de yearth ebry time you sots dem down, and I'se been heah lookin' at dem sparks fur ten minutes, and dey sho' is dar."

After arriving in Savannah, we gave a private exhibition in the dining-room of the Pulaski House, to some twenty or thirty citizens. This proved everywhere to be one of the best modes of advertising. We desired the most respected citizens to see a private exhibiton, that they might be reliable witnesses of the genuineness and good faith of our performances. There were present at this exhibition Congressman Lester, then mayor of the city, Ex-Senator Thomas M. Norwood, Hon. F. G. duBignon, Dr. Wm. Duncan, Dr. J. T. McFarland, Hon. A. P. Adams, Hon. W. D. Harden, Hon. Robt. Falligant, Hon. Marmaduke Hamilton, Maj. W. F. Smythe, Maj. C. C. Hardwick, and a number of others. The entertainment created much excitement, the *Morning News* giving it a two-column write-up, which closed as follows:

"The force which the young lady possesses in so remarkable a degree, and which she does not understand and is unable to control, is called by a number of scientific gentlemen a psychic force, an emanation from the mind and a prolongation of the will, something which has never been analyzed, but which has nothing to do with the supernatural or so-called spiritual."

Senator Norwood was intensely interested in the " Power," and asked for a demontration of the weird "table rapping" test. It would be next to impossible to depict his astonishment. The mysterious raps and the way they answered his questions and manifested intelligence and superior knowledge, were marvelous to him. During the performance at the opera-house the following night he came on the stage and made a speech to the audience, and among other things, told them of the wonderful "raps," and then requested that we introduce this test to the audience, but we explained that we could not, for the raps were not sufficiently loud to be heard over the house. They could have been heard on the stage and out into the orchestra, but would not extend into the main body of the house, and for this reason, but mainly for others which I will give later on, we could not comply with his request.

After leaving Georgia we went into South Carolina. During our trip through the Palmetto State and into the East, we were ably assisted by that enterprising gentleman, Mr. Sanford Cohen, manager of the Augusta Opera House, and who, in 1892, was one of the moving spirits in Atlanta's Exposition. He is a man of wonderful energy and perseverance, and whatever he undertakes he goes into with his whole heart and soul. Our first exhibition was given in the quaint, historic and hospitable city of Charleston. There we gave three or four entertainments to large audiences, and created the greatest excitement. We also gave a private exhibition to the faculty and students of the Medical College. "The following distinguished gentlemen were present, and a more notable and critical audience could hardly be found," said the *News and Courier*. "And we doubt if a more able and scientific body of men ever assembled in the State. There were present more than forty prominent physicians, among them: Drs. J. P. Chazal, I. Ford Prioleau, C. N. Shepard, Jr., F. L. Parker, J. S. Buist, H. D. Fraser, H. W. DeSaussure, F. Peyre Porcher, John Forrest, T. Grange Simons, A. P. Pelzer, W. G. Ogier, P. Gourdin DeSaussure, F. L. Frost, C. B. Lannean, W. P. Porcher, Jno. L. Dawson, W. T. Wragg, R. L. Brodie, John S. Mitchell, R. A. Kinloch, W. H. Huger, Manning Simons, Thomas Legare, E. V. Ivy of California, W. W. Anderson of Sumter county, Dr. Flagg of Georgetown, Dr. Kolloch, Prof. S. W. Johnson of Yale College, Dr. E. H. Jenkins of the Connecticut Agricultural Station, Dr. A. T. Nealle of the New Jersey Agricultural Station, Dr. Middleton Michel, Alderman Rogers, Mr. B. F. Moise, Mr. E. L. Roche, Mr. Bernard O'Neil, Col. Frank E. Taylor, the managers and nearly the entire staff of the *News and Courier*, and many others." The article is a very lengthy one, going into a description of all the tests minutely, and concludes, "There was not a man in this distinguished and learned array who could explain the mysterious phenomenon." This splendid newspaper, the *News and Courier*, was my warm friend, and published many extensive and thrilling articles about me, which carried my fame to every part of the State.

In conclusion, I will quote one of these articles more fully :

"About seven months ago the newspapers began to talk. about Lulu Hurst, a wonderful phenomenon that had appeared near the quiet village of Cedartown, in Polk county, Georgia. The fame of the young lady has spread over the whole country, and the most astounding stories have been told of the peculiar manifestations of her marvelous power. It has been called 'electrical power,' 'animal magnetism,' 'spiritualistic manifestation,' 'psychic force,' but what it is no one knows, and how it acts is yet a profound mystery. It has baffled the wisdom of the most learned physicians and eluded the grasp of the scientists who revel in the unknowable. And the more the public talks the greater the wonder grows. * * * * * * * *

"Lulu Hurst is the talk of the town. The story of her wonderful feats was the most absorbing topic of conversation all over the city yesterday, and the curiosity of the public was excited to the utmost. The physicians who were present at the private performance in the Medical College on Tuesday afternoon were met at every turn by those who wanted to know whether it was really true that the Georgia girl possessed the phenomenal power attributed to her. Ever so many men on Broad street, which as every one knows, is a place especially devoted to abstruse speculations, attempted to account for the mysterious influence by which the Polk county prodigy performed her feats, but the explanation was even more difficult than the occult powers they were designed to illuminate.

"Such was the interest awakened in the matter that Hibernian Hall was filled last night by the largest and most skeptical audience that has ever assembled in Charleston. Every seat was taken, and the closest attention was paid to the performances on the stage, upon which there poured a perfect flood of light. There was no chance for any deception as to how the thing was done, as the stage was open to the audience in front, and the rear and sides of the stage were occupied by a row of gentlemen, all of whom were citizens of Charleston, and were eager to catch at the slightest evidence of foul play.

' * * * * * * * * * *

"It has been a good many years since Charleston has been so stirred up as it has been during the past two days by the strange and inexplicable feats of Lulu Hurst, the laughing phenomenal girl of Georgia. The main topic of conversation yesterday on Broad street and at most of the haunts of men was Lulu Hurst and her wonderful power, and the excitement culminated last night in another crowded audience in Hibernian Hall. The audience embraced representatives from every class in the community; silver-haired sages and beardless boys, grandames, middle-aged matrons and blushing maidens, and a more perplexed and better pleased audience has probably never been gathered in the Hall. The program of the preceding evening was repeated with equally wonderful results. Muscular men swayed to and fro at the will of the Georgia phenomenon, whose merry laughter went far to console them for the rough physical treatment they received at her hands. Miss Hurst is remarkably cheerful and pleasant, and seems to find as much pleasure and enjoyment in the exercise of her strange powers as is afforded to her audiences."

From Charleston we visited the principal towns of the State. We gave an exhibition in Columbia. There were on the stage to test the "Power" here, Major John T. Rhett, Ex-Mayor W. B. Stanley, Col. A. C. Haskell, Col. Jas. H. Rion, Col. J. P. Richardson, Capt. C. J. Iredell, Capt. Willie Jones, Mr. N. G. Gonzales, and others. Here happened a sad and severe accident. Col. James H. Rion, a lawyer of State reputation, in attempting to hold a chair when I placed my hands upon it, bursted a blood-vessel in his arm. Blood poison ensued, and for days his life hung in a balance. There was great anxiety all over the State about his condition, for he was to South Carolina what Judge Marshall Clarke was to my native State. We were greatly delighted when we heard of Col. Rion's recovery some time thereafter.

By this time my fame had grown to such an extent that various manufactured articles, such as brands of tobacco, cigars, soap, etc., etc., had been given my name. Various articles were sent to me as compliments with my name branded on them. Near Columbia, S. C., was a large Jersey farm, and the proprietor insisted on driving us out and showing us the beautiful and select herd of cattle. One of the choicest of his young cows had been registered "Lulu Hurst." My father was so charmed with her qualities and appearance that he purchased her at a fancy price and shipped her to his plantation in Georgia.

From this State we entered North Carolina, but did not give many exhibitions here, for (I say it not boastfully) my fame had become so widely known that my management thought best to hurry to the North and East. So we bade adieu to the delightful and hospitable people of the beautiful Southland to try our fortunes and the success of the power among those who were strangers to us.

CHAPTER X.

THE "POWER" IN THE NATIONAL CAPITAL.

The "Force" Tested by the Savants of the Smithsonian Institute—The Mystery Deepens—Senator John B. Gordon Goes Down in Defeat—Congressmen Succumb to the Inevitable—A Private Exhibition to Scientists in the Laboratory of Prof. Bell.

Since the establishment of American independence, the "Georgia Wonder" is the only Power that ever invaded the national capital, established headquarters there, and successfully defied and overthrew every force sent against it. Moreover, this "Power" not only met and conquered the ordinary militia and reserves of the nation, which came against it, but it took captive the greatest military and civic leaders of the nation quartered there, and defied the engineering skill and improved scientific defenses provided by the government corps stationed in the great Smithsonian Institute and Naval Observatory.

Begging pardon of the reader for the grandiloquent style of the above statements, I desire to say in an humbler and simpler vein that the "Power" conquered Washington.

My success there marked a very important epoch in the

career of the "Force." For Washington was the gateway
into the North and East, and when I left this city I found
my fame fully established wherever I went.

In order to keep this volume in the reasonable limits I
intend to have it, I can only give cursory accounts of my
various entertainments and incidents connected therewith.
The reader has observed that I have but seldom gone into
details as to the tests, and the exciting stage experiences of
my performances. This would be tedious and prolix, as
the tests used and the feats performed were the same that I
described in the beginning. But, I ought to state by way
of explanation, that at almost every performance there were
new and different variations in the behavior and conduct
of the subjects, while under the tyrannical dominion of the
"Power."

The effect and influence of the "Force" on different
ones was entirely beyond my control. One man would
show no agitation, and would struggle bravely and go down
on his head or back in defeat manfully, and show no fear
of the mysterious power. Another would come up to test
it with the "horrors" written all over his face and the St.
Vitus dance in his legs, even before the force got hold of
him. I would know when I looked at him, that nothing
but the walls and the wings and the roof of the stage would
save him from a flight off into space. I often felt real pity
for these kind of victims, for I knew they stood in awe of
the mystery, and nothing but their morbid curiosity could
have led them captive to the slaughter.

I could see in the face of another that he had come to
defy the "Power," believing nothing of it, and wishing to
expose it, and thinking he could do so. But, as a general

rule, even these skeptics soon showed "confusion worse confounded." Often, in such cases, the "Power" came upon them by a more circuitous route, augmenting itself by mysterious degrees and taking hold of them unawares. When the strange influence began to assert itself, they would begin to show it by a peculiar, funny "squat" like an overpowering weight had been placed upon their shoulders. Then they would straighten up and get a firmer brace. Then they would lose their balance and step forward or backward. Then the reaction from this position would come, which would result in their going suddenly over in the opposite direction. They would then cast their eyes behind them to see if some one had not pushed them, and seeing no one their doubts would begin to dissipate and the mystery to deepen. Then the "war dance" would begin. Their feet would beat a quick and wild tattoo on the stage, and their bodies would sway to and fro to the time of their "quick-step"—then the end quickly came, and these doubting warriors would measure their martial dimensions on the floor. Others claimed that they could feel the very presence of an invisible band of spirits hovering about them, and their movements were, as they supposed, in harmony and touch with these invisibles. It was thus in different ways, the subjects who tested the power would manifest its effect upon them. Very few acted exactly alike.

Quite often they would try to explain to the audience the effect of the power on them. Some said it seemed to come out of the object itself which they were trying to hold. Others said it seemed that they themselves would become, as it were, partially paralized, and an overpowering influence seemed to take possession of their bodies that rendered them powerless. Others said they experienced a violent electric shock that benumbed them, and took away their strength. Then others likened the force to that of an engine or other powerful mechanical instrument that was absolutely irresistible. Some said the force came gently at first like the swaying of a leaf by a zephyr and ended like a cataclysm, or the mighty burst of a storm.

Still others said they collapsed at once, as though an electric bolt had struck them. And thus everywhere the influence caused people to act and talk differently about it.

After arriving in Washington, the metropolitan press wrote up the "Georgia Wonder" in modern sensational style. They gave me all the advertising we could wish for. We exhibited here for a week or ten days to large and enthusiastic audiences. We were guests of the Metropolitan Hotel, the home of many Southern congressmen and senators. These gallant gentlemen took great interest in my power, and, I might say with becoming modesty, in me.

During our stay in Washington we gave a private exhibition in the parlors of the Metropolitan Hotel. The rooms were crowded with visitors. The scientists were there in full force, and the newspapers not only of Washington but of New York City, Chicago, Philadelphia and other cities had their representatives there. Among the large number of senators and congressmen present I remember the following:

Senator Ransom, Senator Gordon of Georgia, Congressmen Willitts, Blount, Reese and Clements. There were many other noted gentlemen present, including Richard Townshend. I never will forget how it impressed me, as a girl, to see how my Power behaved at this noted exhibition. There was such a want of reverence and discrimination in it. It was no respecter of persons. Think of our gallant General John B. Gordon being paralyzed by it, and allowing it to cause his martial figure to retreat hither and thither, skirting the walls of the room for defense and protection; he who rarely beat a retreat before the bravest armies, flying before this power in the most demoralized fashion.

The distinguished members of the Smithsonian Institute and Naval Observatory, together with other scientists, arranged for a private exhibition at the laboratory of Prof. Bell, the world-renowned inventor of the telephone. I spent a day with these distinguished men, some twenty or more of them, and they conducted all sorts of tests with me. They insulated me by putting me on a platform supported by glass rods. They claimed that if the power was electrical it would not operate when insulated in this manner. But this had no effect on it. They placed me upon a pair of scales. My weight was then ascertained. They then pushed the scale pea out until it showed twenty pounds more than my actual weight. They then placed a gentleman weighing two hundred pounds in a chair near the scales, I still remaining on the platform; then they asked me to try and lift the chair and gentleman. I did so, and yet strange to say, the scale beam remained undisturbed. In other words, with a margin of only twenty pounds, I raised a weight of two hundred pounds, and did not consume even the twenty pounds on the scales. They were amazed beyond measure, because they here saw, what appeared to be, an utter annihilation of weight. A number of other tests were made, but under them all the power remained as potent as ever. This distinguished company of savants wanted to examine my blood. So they took a drop from my arm, and placed it under their powerful microscope. This specimen created as much interest in their minds as the power. They all declared that no such specimen of blood had ever been seen by them. They pronounced the blood corpuscles absolutely perfect. They mounted and sealed this specimen, and put it on exhibition at the Smithsonian Institute. I suppose it is still there, where it can be seen to this day.

Among the number of distinguished men at this exhibition, I can recall the following names:

Prof. Bell, Prof. Newcome, Prof. Hilgard, Prof. Taylor of the Smithsonian Institute, and Prof. John R. Eastman of the Naval Observatory.

Prof. Bell was intensely interested in me and made another engagement with me at the Metropolitan Hotel. Here he continued his investigations and tests of one sort and another, but without arriving at any solution. This great investigator and discoverer could girdle the earth with the human voice, and annihilate space and time between man and man, but he went down in defeat before the "Power," and left it as he had found it, shrouded in a mystery unfathomed and apparently unfathomable.

While in Washington we made a visit to the United States treasury. We had as a chaperone and companion that prince among clever gentlemen, H. W. J. Ham, of Gainesville, Georgia, he of "Snollygoster" fame. This visit to the treasury vaults had a funny turn to it. When we reached the vaults, the guards knew who we were, and they expressed some doubt as to the advisability of letting me get near the money bags; I suppose they were afraid I might work the power on the bags of gold and "spirit" some of them away.

In many respects I consider my experiences in Washington the most important of my career.

When I went before the learned bodies who examined me there, I went feeling that they would be able to explain to me the things that I was wholly unable to account for or explain. While I was convinced there was a solution to the mystery, I was at a loss to account for the many strange and apparently inexplicable features connected with it, yet I felt that when the solution was reached it would be found within the realm of cause and effect; and though I was unable to account for a great many things in connection with it, yet I must say that the mystery, instead of being cleared away, was only deepened by the utter inability of these learned men to give me any light on the subject. The only thing they accomplished was to make certain tests to prove by exclusion what it was not, but they never were able to tell what it was. Among the number who took part in the examination, there was but one who doubted that the power was a genuine, occult phenomenon, or, in other words, there was but one skeptic, and that was Prof. Newcome. I had gone there expecting these savants, these scholars, who stand at the head of the scientific department of the government, to give me light, but, when we got through, it was like the blind leading the blind; we all fell into the ditch. In all my travels in the South wherever I had gone, I had submitted my "Power" to scientific and medical men, singly and in bodies, that they might solve the mystery so strangely connected with my person or personality—but in vain. When I came to this seat of learning, this Modern Athens of America, I expected myself and the world to be enlightened as to the mystery, and to be informed of the "Great Secret."

Some investigators had told me that I hypnotized the people who came before me to test the power, and that I had no other power. But these savants said it was not hypnotism. Others had said that what I did was by legerdemain, but, if so, these scientists failed to expose it for the benefit of the world, though they adopted every precaution to do so.

Still others had affirmed that the power was electrical or magnetic, but with every appliance known to science, this college of investigators had sought for electric and magnetic forces, and found none. It was affirmed by some that the force was muscular and the feats performed by clever muscular manipulation, but these men and many other trained observers repudiated this explanation.

During my tests, when the greatest exertion of muscular force would have been required to accomplish the results, they affirmed that there was no pressure under my hands, and no contraction or tension of the muscles of my arms, and after long-continued and laborious feats, when those who tested my power were exhausted by their efforts to oppose it, it was found that my pulse and respiration were normal in every way, and no other perceptible sign of exertion by me. Others argued that if muscular power was used, it would at once show it on the scales, but to all appearances, under my touch weight was annihilated and sixteen ounces refused to be a pound.

These repeated failures to explain the mystery, but left it in deeper darkness than had ever before enveloped it. I, myself, was not at an age to reason much about it, or to attempt to give any scientific opinion or other explanation.

There were those who called it "Odic Force," but what they meant was as much a mystery to me as the thing itself; and some classed it "Psychic Force," which term to my mind was the same as if they had said they did not know what it was. There were others who contended that the force was only a "Prolongation of the Will;" this too was an explanation that failed to explain. The spiritulists everywhere said it was all to be accounted for as Spirit Phenomena, but I repelled such a superstitious idea as this.

So I left the great city of Washington as much in the dark as I was when I went there.

I give a quotation below from a scholarly and thoughtful essay by one of these eminent scientists, which, at the time, was very extensively copied in the journals of the continent :

"In Miss Hurst's case the muscles and nerves conduct a force not generated within them. It is said that objects at a distance sometimes move from place to place in response to her volition. I see no reason to discredit this statement, after somewhat large experience with phenomena of a similar character. I do not, however, consider her will a source of energy in such a case, much less that a disengagement of the force from the muscles moves the object. How could such a force make contact with and adhere to the object when she does not touch it? But it may be said that Miss Hurst has given no such exhibition in public.

Possibly not. But Angelique Cottin, in Paris, somewhere about 1835, gave such exhibitions before certain savants of that city, among whom was Arago. Physical objects in her presence were moved with tremendous force, when it was quite clear to the observers that she had no physical contact with them. The popular cry was that the phenomena were produced by electricity. But no electrometer in the hands of the savants was delicate enough to detect it. It was after having witnessed these phenomena that Arago is said to have remarked : *'Gentlemen, he is a bold man who outside of mathematics, ventures to utter the word—impossible.'*

"If, as is alleged, the movement of physical objects sometimes occurs in Miss Hurst's presence without her personal contact with them, but in response to her volition, we must logically infer a force not muscular. Mental volitions do not direct force; they do not generate it. A mental volition sets up a decomposition of muscular and nervous tissues, and the force with which one moves a hand or an arm is thus evolved and discharged. But no mortal can effect a control of this kind of force with a physical object, unless some bodily organ is in contact with such object. The forces coming through the person of Miss Hurst can achieve a contact at times with physical objects, when she has no personal contact with them. This is the beautiful mystery incidental to her phenomenon. She is another Angelique Cottin. We have named that form of electricity evolved from decomposing copper and zinc (when, decomposing in contact) galvanism, from Dr. Galvani. Why not call the new force evolved in Miss Hurst's presence, Lulism or Cottinism. The name will serve as an objective *point de mere* toward which our studies and speculations in regard to the new force may converge. It will be time enough to call it muscular force when we have come to believe that the electric current that shatters a church steeple should be called steeple force, and that it is evolved from the weather-cock."

CHAPTER XI.

ADIEU TO WASHINGTON.

Into Maryland and New Jersey—Mr. Chas. Frohman, the Great Theatrical Manager, Takes Charge of the Power—"The Great Unknown" in New York City—The First Night at Wallack's—The Power is All-Powerful—Giant Club Men Succumb—The Voice of the Press—The Mesmerist Lubin and the Athlete Lafflin in the Throes of the Force.

When we bade adieu to Washington, and left behind us its wealth, its politics, its civic and national grandeur, its vast and magnificent architectural beauty, I carried with me the memories and experiences, not so much of these things, but of a character never felt or known, perhaps, by another than myself, since this famous metropolis was founded. Though but a girl of immature years, my experiences there had caused me to realize more than ever that I occupied before the world an absolutely unique position, different at that time from all the millions of people who lived and moved about me. Of course this reflection did not impress me then as much as it came to do in subsequent years after I had left the stage, but I felt it more forcibly than ever before. The confessed failure of the large number of learned men, who experimented with me there, to throw some light upon the deep mystery of my power, weighed upon me, and in some measure was depressing to me. I had reached a point where I wanted the "mystery" solved, and solved not only for myself but for the world. For I had begun to see some of the effects it was beginning to have on the minds of the people in creating superstitious ideas and hurtful delusions.

I had hoped to see this "Force" (so mysteriously connected with myself and considered by everybody as allied with the unreal and occult) properly understood and classified by the scientists, as only an unusul phase of some known, natural and normal element. But the investigations there ended only in failure and collapse as all others had done.

Then and there I formed this resolution: If possible, I will solve this mystery myself. I will find out just how the force proceeding from me accomplishes the wonders it performs. I will see if I can reduce it to the category of known and demonstrable phenomena, and when I do this to my satisfaction, if ever I do, I will give the explanation to the public.

So, having fixed this resolution firmly in my mind, I calmed myself with that species of satisfaction that one feels when one determines to do the best they can under all circumstances.

*   *   *   *   *   *

From Washington we went to Baltimore, Md., and there exhibited for a week or ten days at Ford's splendid theater. Hundreds of the leading citizens of this beautiful city tested the power, and thousands witnessed the performances. There was nothing to distinguish these exhibitions from many others we had given all over the country. There was the same enthusiam, the same astonishment and insatiable curiosity about the wonderful force.

One noticeable feature of our Baltimore audiences was the large number of commercial travelers whom I had met during our exhibitions farther south. Many of the staunchest friends we made during our stage experiences were drummers. I always found them invariably clever, courteous and intelligent, and they were ever ready to defend the "Power" whenever it was assailed or doubted. As a rule I found them to be a splendid class of gentlemen.

On the first night of our engagement in Baltimore, there was a young man who came on the stage in company with a number of others, who came upon our invitation to test the "Power." He watched the performance very closely and seemed to take a deep interest in all the tests, although he participated in none of them.

After the exhibition he introduced himself, and was none other than Mr. Chas. Frohman, the great theatrical manager. He was so well pleased that he at once sought the opportunity to close a contract for my appearance in New York city. Terms were agreed upon, and we got into the hands of one of the most enterprising and successful theatrical managers on the continent.

From Baltimore we went to Hagerstown, Columbia, Patterson, Trenton, and other cities, and thence on to New York city.

Mr. Frohman felt so confident of the success that would attend our unique performances, and was so sure it would startle and amaze the New Yorkers, just as it had done everybody else, that he secured one of the finest theaters in the city for our exhibitions, the famous "Wallack's."

Our first exhibition here was a private exhibition to the press, and was witnessed by representatives from all the metropolitan papers. An unfortunate accident occurred at this exhibition, which came very near causing my manager to lose one of his eyes. It occurred in this way: Mr. Banks Winters, the famous tenor singer, and the author of beautiful "White Wings," was trying to hold the umbrella. The "Power" was unusually unruly, and was about to carry him off the stage when my manager rushed forward to catch him, and, as he did so, the collapse came, and one of the ribs of the ill-fated umbrella struck him just under the eye, penetrating into the bone. Physicians present attended him, but his vision was impaired for a long time. Excepting this unfortunate accident the exhibition was a great success, and so written up in all of the papers.

It would be a waste of words for me to expatiate on what my fame was in the great city, even before I had given my first public entertainment there. I say it without boasting, the name of the "Georgia Wonder" was in everybody's mouth. The people in that theater-going city were hungry for something new. They had been satiated with the real; they wanted the *"unreal."* They had been fed on all kinds of humanly devised novelties. They yearned for one unique, mysterious, standing alone, and, as it were, far above others, like the great pyramid of Gizeh in the desert towers solitary above its fellows. They had time and again had phenomena of *art;* they cried for phenomena of *nature.* From all accounts they had seen, and there had been many weird and extravagant articles in the metropolitan press, there was now in their midst a real "Wonder," and a "Wonder" of the "Unreal," fresh

61

from the hidden realms of nature's unseen and unknown phenomena.

It was thus that we found the public expectancy. Mr. Frohman had divined this state of affairs before he came to Baltimore to make us a proposal for our appearance in the great Metropolis of the New World. Our first exhibition was given there July 8, 1884. I can never forget our anxiety, my own and that of the manager's, before the entertainment began that memorable night. When the hour for the performance arrived every seat in the great theater was filled. The boxes were occupied, and from pit to dome was a packed mass of humanity. My management realized, and so did I, that if the exhibition of the first night was a success, the success of our entire engagement was assured. And on whom did the burden of all this enterprise depend? Who must entertain that vast crowd of humanity, composed of people learned and unlearned, cultured and ignorant, refined and coarse, wealthy and poor, elegant and inelegant—all critical, expectant and clamorous for wonders, yet skeptical to the last degree? Who must enthuse them, excite their admiration, and then their wonder, and satisfy all? Was it I, myself, *alone;* a country lass of fifteen summers, whose days had been spent until recently upon a quiet Georgia farm—who had never known anything of the world's wily ways, nor of schemes and cunning and strategy and plots—forces that are generated in the womb of social warfare, and grow strong in the battle for pelf, profit, position and power?

No, it was not this inexperienced country girl—*alone.* The case was worse than that, for I was not expected to entertain as a clown or a buffoon, or a country clog-dancer or a mere prestidigitator. These people "sought for a sign," and from some unknown realm or wonderland of the great unexplored abyss of the universe, where human foot had never trodden, nor eye penetrated, nor ear heard, nor brain conceived, I was expected to bring forth unimagined wonders!

It was not I alone; it was a "Force,'" an inscrutible "Power," which I must be able to conjure up from the vasty deep, to call forth from this abyss of the Unknown and command it to do my bidding. Suppose it should disobey me to-night, elude me, defy me, leave me helpless and wonderless and powerless and forceless, at the mercy of that gaping crowd? They did not come to see me alone, but "It."

Think of their disappointment, their rage, their jests, their contumely, and of my humiliation and despair, if the "Unknown" should desert me to-night! Thus we stood, face to face—that vast, eager audience, and the girl! Would "The Great Unknown" come? Was "It" already there to do my bidding? Would "It" desert me this time, or prove "Itself" truer and more wonderful than ever? It is time for the curtain to rise. We must see; we must try beforehand, and not go down in defeat before the vast audience. I called my manager and my father. The decisive tests for the power were made in almost breathless anxiety, and lo! "It" was there. We then called for the curtain, and I and "It" faced the greatest audience we had ever met and defied!

* * * * * * * * *

Among some of the prominent personages there that night, I remember the following:

Ex-Senator Roscoe Conkling, Gen. Dan Sickles, Rev.
Dr. Hepworth, John T. Raymond, Dr. Henry A. Mott,
Prof. Jas. Lafflin, Mrs. Langtry, Bartley Campbell, Miss
Georgia Cayvan, W. H. Vanderbilt, Billy Edwards, Harry
Hill, and hundreds of others.

It would be impossible for me to describe the success of
this performance.   Language could never portray the wild
enthusiasm, the uproarious "tumult," the frantic demeanor of
that audience, when the Power hurled defiance full in their
face, and crushed without mercy every human force that
came against it!   As one company and battalion of men
after another went down in utter defeat before me, the
audience yelled and shrieked and stamped their feet and
threw up their hats, etc., and an unquellable pandemonium
took possession of them.   At times every person in the
house—man, woman and child—seemed to be on their feet,
waving their hats, handkerchiefs, etc., and a wild frenzy of
enthusiasm seemed to have taken possession of them!

We were told afterwards that no such demonstration of
applause had ever been seen there.   I was forced time and
again to acknowledge the generous applause.

The people were so aroused, and the success of the entertainment so great, that after the exhibition hundreds flocked
to the stage to see me and speak to me.   Among this number was that "greatest business woman of the continent,"
Mrs. Frank Leslie, with one of her artists, who made some
sketches which were afterwards produced in her famous
magazine.

When I went out of the theater I found hundreds on the
streets awaiting my appearance.

When we arrived at our hotel there were some thirty or

forty newspaper reporters awaiting my arrival. I was only too glad to give them an interview, and also let them test the power until they were fully satisfied that they were in the presence of a "Great Unknown Force." The consequence was, we did not get to bed until near morning, and then I awoke to find that I was indeed famous.

I give at the close of this chapter some quotations from the metropolitan press as a sample of hundreds of columns that were written in New York city about my entertainments there.

I was much impressed and amused afterwards by Mr. Chas. Frohman's comments on this first night's performance. He said that he got a seat in one of the upper boxes where he could watch the audience, and when he looked over the immense assemblage he, for the first time, fully realized the great risk he had assumed in bringing a young girl there to make a performance, and when this stripling of a girl arose to make the first test, his heart almost stopped beating. But when the "Power" began to get in its work and the great audience to show its approval and enthusiasm, his courage began to return, and when the performance was half over he said he was just as much interested in it as was the audience. Well do I remember when the curtain went down how he rushed upon the stage and showered his congratulations upon me!

Our first night in New York was over, and with it our success was doubly assured.

"The Great Unknown" did not desert me.

* * * *

The New York *Times* gave a column or more in describing the exhibition with the following head-lines:

"STRONG MEN CHILDREN IN IIER HANDS."

" Twenty Club Athletes Retire Discomfited"—"Lulu Hurst Moves them Around at Will"—"A Distinguished Gathering"—"Mr. Vanderbilt Wants an Exhibition, Etc."

The *Graphic* says: "An excited multitude occupied Wallack's Theater last night, drawn thither by Miss Lulu Hurst's remarkable exhibition. It expresses it mildly to say that she created a tremendous furor, and that those who were present went away either completely mystified or filled with thought. * * * * * * *

"She has opened up a field of speculation worthy the attention of neurologists. Pathologists should certainly see her and try to discover whether they could not suggest something new for the benefit of humanity in this girl endowed with such marvelous magnetism. She proves that we are on the verge of some new discovery in vital human forces, and scientists should be inquisitive rather than testy and skillful. * * * * * * *

" Miss Hurst is a marvel and must be investigated."

The following account from the *Telegram* I will quote more at length as it gives a description of the tests made with the veteran prestidigitator and mesmerist, Mr. Fred Lubin, and the great athlete, Professor Lafflin :

" The most remarkable production of the season, so far, is Miss Lulu Hurst, the young lady that comes from Georgia. After astounding a number of newspaper men on Saturday afternoon, she made her first public appearance before a large audience at Wallack's Theater on Monday evening. Whenever anything happens that is not explainable, there are apt to be skeptics. As the audience left the theater after the performance, fully three-fourths were doubtful of the reasons which produced such remarkable results, but no one could explain them. The theories advanced were curious to listen to. If the power possessed by this young lady is really a magnetic or electric force, then it is most remarkable. If it is muscular power, then it is *more remarkable still;* and if it is a trick, then *it is more wonderful still that nobody has yet been able to explain it or see through it.*

"The veteran prestidigitator and mesmerist, Mr. Fred Lubin, went to Wallack's determined to show up the humbug. Nobody could fool him. The athlete Lafflin went there intent upon proving that, however great might be her physical power, she could not outdo him. Several other gentlemen who were always cocksure about everything also visited Wallack's, premising their visit with the statement that while she might be able to humbug a lot of newspaper men, *they* would soon be able to expose her to the broad glare of public derision and contempt.

"All these gentlemen went upon the stage to try their power against her. Mr. Lubin carefully examined the umbrella which he was asked to hold. Then he demanded another in the audience, so as to convince the people that he was not to be taken in by any prepared mechanism.

"Then he stood under the umbrella with Miss Hurst facing him. He held the handle with his two clinched hands. Miss Hurst touched the handle with her open palm and in a moment Mr. Lubin was cavorting about the stage like a marionette on springs, and suddenly the umbrella was wrenched from his hands and lay a twisted, shapeless mass upon the stage. Mr. Lubin looked puzzled and serious. He tried again with the same result. Mr. Lafflin

took a billiard cue in his hands, braced himself firmly on
his legs, the intensity of his clutch on the cue making the
muscles of his arms stand out like lumps of hard rubber.
Miss Hurst stood before him, placed her right hand on the
cue, passed her left through her hair, and then placed the
fingers of her left hand on the cue.   Mr. Lafflin began to
sway from side to side, then staggered, and then began to
move in violent contortions about the stage, Miss Hurst
keeping her open hand on the cue.   Suddenly Mr. Lafflin
gave way, then turned half around, and fell in a heap in a
corner, displacing several chairs.   The audience was intensely wrought up and their excitement utterly beyond
control.   Then Mr. Lafflin took a firm hold on a chair
and held it four feet from the floor.   Miss Hurst placed
two fingers and a thumb lightly on Mr. Lafflin's hands,
the two smaller fingers of each hand being on the chair.
In a moment Mr. Lafflin again staggered about the stage.
He let go and the chair bounded off and struck a piece of
scenery four feet from the floor and fell.   Again Mr. Lafflin
took his hold on the chair, and was requested to put it on
the floor, Miss Hurst again placing her hands on his.   He
could not get it within more than a foot of the stage.   Mr.
Lubin was invited to come and help the other, and together
they struggled with no better results.   Then a third, a
fourth, a fifth, a sixth and eventually eight portly gentlemen came to the rescue, and pressed with all their might,
but Miss Hurst's hands were still on Mr. Lafflin's, and
while the chair moved in concentric circles, horizontally,
the mass of weight could not move it downward.   Finally
and suddenly, Miss Hurst took her hands off the chair,
and they tumbled on top of one another, while her silvery
laugh rang out above the din they made."

CHAPTER XII.

NEW YORK IN THE FOILS OF "THE UNKNOWN."

A Riot Imminent—Chief of Police Williamson to the Rescue—A Score of Columns a Day in the Metropolitan Press Concerning "The Great Unknown"—Dr. W. E. Forest, the Skeptic, Routed—Scenes Never to be Forgotten.

My first night in New York was not simply a success; it proved a veritable landslide, or an avalanche. The next morning all the great daily papers came out with long accounts of the first performance, a few of which I have given. Many of these accounts were of a column or more and very glowing and sensational. To show the interest taken in my "Power," I will state, on authority of those who had every opportunity to judge and to know, that while I was in New York the press published more literature about myself and the "Unknown" and our performances than was ever written concerning any other performance or entertainment ever seen in the city. I do not mention this in a spirit of vanity, but only to give an idea of the overwhelming interest taken in the "Great Unknown." I was overrun in every conceivable way by the sensation-hunters, reporters for every kind of paper, reviewers, requests for private entertainments by wealthy men and women, spiritualists seeking in me a Moses or a St. Paul of their faith, and cranks of all kinds and characters.

For awhile I gave audience to all these people, but I soon found out that if I did not stop it, I would have no time of my own, and I had to become more exclusive. But I was " rushed " in this way the whole time I remained in the great city.

Well, when the public read the papers the next morning, they began to wake up to the fact that there must be a real, genuine "Wonder" in their midst after all. If the papers left anything unsaid the public added it from their imagination, so that on the second night standing room at Wallack's was at a premium. The performance this night was more exciting than on the first night on account of a disturbance which came near resulting in a riot. One Dr. W. E. Forest came on the stage with others to test the power. He refused to comply with my manager's request to hold the objects so they would not endanger me, but insisted on doing it his own way. Because my manager objected he asserted the power was a fraud and that he could duplicate the performance. He was so discourteous with it all that the audience became overwhelmingly in sympathy with me. He persisted in his interruption, and the audience became frantic with him, and a hundred or more men rushed to the stage and espoused the cause of the "Power." The chief of police, Capt. Williamson, who was already on the stage, succeeded in quelling the disturbance without any one being hurt.

The following reports will give an idea of the excitement attending this performance :

New York Daily Tribune:

"Pandemonium reigned last night at Wallack's. A house full of people were yelling and hooting till apoplectic-looking faces were the rule and not the exception.

"Men were standing up so as to give their lungs free play, and women were screaming and waving handkerchiefs in their excitement. Viewed over the glare of the footlights, the sight of tier after tier of packed humanity possessed of a sudden frenzy was a striking one. Up to this point the entertainment by the 'Georgia Wonder' had gone on in the usual way. She had made a man's forehead bleed with the ferocious umbrella; she had led 'Harry' Hill a dance about the stage, and she had twisted Mr. De Mille of the Madison Square theater as though he had been a reed in her hands. When a well-known member of the New York Athletic Club grasped the chair firmly, Miss Hurst laid her hand upon it and it flew about the stage with the athlete after it.

"Then the tall man with the beard arose and stalked solemnly down to the footlights. He picked up the chair, and instead of holding it closely to his body as the others had done, he held it a little way from him. Miss Hurst put her hands on it and it jumped up and hit her on the chin. The manager rushed forward and motioned the tall man away. He objected; the spectators yelled and hissed at him. The manager insisted that he must hold the chair so as not to endanger the young lady, and it was dangerous to her if held as he insisted on holding it. The spectators yelled and shrieked and hissed, and finally quiet was restored, and the skeptic induced to retire by a man in blue uniform and white helmet who owes allegiance to Capt. Williamson of the 29th precinct.

"Later the skeptic came back, and when others on the stage were giving their experience with the power, he attempted to speak, but the audience cried him down and ordered him to hire a hall for himself. *   *   *

"Finally, in the height of the excitement the curtain went down.   The only calm and collected person in the entire building was Miss Lulu Hurst."

The World Says:

"Twelve hundred excited individuals howled themselves hoarse last night at Wallack's theater. Wall street brokers, Union Club men, ladies from Fifth avenue, toughs from the Bowery and sporting men from Harry Hill's precinct yelled and sputtered and screamed for nearly an hour. Miss Lulu Hurst, the Georgia wonder, and one Dr. Forest, who attempted to expose her, were at the bottom of the row.

*   *   *   *   *

"'Go hire a hall for yourself if you want to give a show.' 'Put him out!' 'Where are the police!' greeted the physician, and the noise redoubled as a big policeman took the doctor's arm. 'Get off the stage!' 'Come off, come off!' finally resolved itself into a grand chorus, and the doctor hid himself in an orchestra chair."

Dr. Forest's discourteous manner of conducting his tests with the "Power" was severely criticised by all the New York papers.   The sympathy of the press was on my side. Even the physicians condemned Dr. Forest.   As a sample I give a card from Dr. J. W. Porter in the *Evening Telegram* of July 10th, 1884.   He writes :

"This evening is the second occasion on which I have been a witness to the phenomenal powers of Miss Lulu Hurst

"The first was a private exhibition where we all had a full and fair opportunity to test her in any way the thirty or forty gentlemen present desired.

"I am quite of the opinion that no gentleman left the theater on that occasion with any idea of any unfairness, and in this connection I may say that the lady's manager, Mr. P. M. Atkinson, came very near losing an eye and received a very severe injury from remaining in too close proximity to her while the umbrella exhibit was in progress. I mention this to say that I do not consider the conduct of Dr. Forest while on the stage this evening as at all proper or just to the lady. He seemed to take the position that he could hold the chair in such a way as was most desirable to himself, while it is perfectly well-known to those who had made like attempts that Miss Hurst is not responsible for the direction the chair will take when it once begins to move; therefore it was quite natural that her manager should ask the doctor to hold the chair in such a position as not to endanger the lady.

"For myself, after every opportunity to see and investigate all of the phenomena presented by Miss Hurst, I am free to say I have no explanation to offer. She is one of the unknown quantities, and will be fully appreciated as such by all reasonable persons when they have once come under the irresistible influence of the mysterious force which, although not under her control, is within her power to call forth.

"I am quite free to say that the audience of last evening expressed their sympathy entirely with her.

(Signed) "J. W. Porter, M.D.,
"Gilsey House."

In this connection I might state that while I was in New York Dr. Hammond, the famous physician, would not or did not come to examine the " Power," but yet gave an opinion that it was a trick aided by extraordinary strength. This aroused a great many of the papers, and Dr. Hammond was severely criticised for such an opinion. The papers, without an exception, acknowledged the genuineness of the " Power," and the absence of trickery and muscular strength. The New York *World* said editorially :

" Dr. Hammond, whose scientific alacrity in giving opinions upon subjects with which he is eminently and proudly ignorant is notorious. He has announced that he has not yet seen the phenomenal girl now on exhibition at Wallack's Theater, but he has no doubt whatever that her performance is a trick aided by extraordinary muscular strength.

" This is altogether rougher on the intelligent public that assembled on Monday night to witness Miss Hurst's performances than it is on the girl herself. To sum up this curious and strange exhibition as a trick, is to condemn that concourse of spectators as the shallowest assemblage of dolts that ever got together.

" As a trick or an exhibition of muscular strength alone, it was simply ridiculous. But the audience saw a not over robust girl of about fifteen overcome with a touch of her hand six struggling and straining athletes, who slipped and stumbled in their excess of endeavor, who panted and sweated in vain, while with relaxed muscles, undisturbed respiration and even pulse, she defied their combined strength. This, Dr. Hammond, from the safe distance of his study, says is undoubtedly a trick. There is no doubt that men who, like Dr. Hammond, are so cock-sure, do a great deal towards making these exhibitions degenerate into real trickery."

The New York *Journal* gave a column account of one of my performances, from which I quote the following:

"Among the dozen or more men seated on the stage were Major J. E. Tolfree of the United States Navy, a large, powerful man of splendid physique, George DeForrest Grant, one of the best trained athletes among the young society men of the city, Howard Lapsley, Elliot Smith and Reginald Francklyn, the bosom friend of Fred Gebhard, and a man of great muscular development. These gentlemen are all members of the Union Club and had come to the theater in a party accompanied by ladies, for the express purpose of testing the powers of the Wonder, and furnishing their friends with their impressions of the seance.

"After several umbrellas had collapsed under the magic of her touch, Major Tolfree was given a stout walking-stick with instructions to grasp it firmly with both hands, hold it steady and remain quiet. Miss Hurst simply rested the palm of her hand against the stick, put the other behind her, looked up at her stalwart adversary with a shy glance, gave a little almost inaudible laugh, and then the gallant major began his war dance. He tried violently to obey orders and keep quiet. Mr. Grant tried to help him, but only made matters worse, and the two became inextricably mixed up in their gyrations about the stage.

"Then Mr. Francklyn attempted to remain stationary with a billiard cue in his terrible grip. He braced himself and said he felt as immovable as the eternal hills. The major sung out to him 'to look out for her when she laughed!' and as he spoke the girl laid her open hand gently on the billiard cue and broke out into a hearty laugh. 'Look out, Regi!' came from Elliot Smith, but Regi could pay little attention to his friend, for he was busy dancing around the stage with Miss Lulu for a partner. As he gave up and took a seat exhausted, he said:

" 'By Jove, that's the most wonderful thing I ever saw, you know, by Jove.' .

" Then Mr. Grant and Mr. Lapsley, two of the strongest men in the Union Club, decided to make the attempt to force the end of the billiard cue to the floor while 'the Wonder' exerted her hidden power to prevent them. They failed, and then came the chair test.

" A fat man was selected and asked to take a seat in a chair placed near the footlights. He did so, saying his weight was 285 pounds. Miss Lulu moved the chair with one of her hands in full view of the audience. It rested upon the side of the chair and did not grasp it. A *Journal* reporter watched the other hand and its position was the same. Miss Lulu bent over, laughed a cherry laugh in the man's ear, and the chair rose from the floor with no apparent exertion on her part. This was repeated with a half dozen heavy weights, and in no instance did 'the Wonder' fail.

" As a closing test the five Union Club men proposed that they all try to force a chair to the floor, holding it between them with their united strength, giving the Wonder just room to rest one hand upon the seat and the other against the back. When all was ready the grand effort began, and slowly and laboriously the chair descended, and

the athletes puffed and blew and strained every nerve.
From the bunch of heads came forth Miss Lulu's merry
laugh, and she raised one hand over her head.   The chair
neared the floor inch by inch, when suddenly the Wonder
withdrew her power and the giants collapsed in a heap on
the floor."

The New York *Times*, in a two-column article, says
among other things :

" Twenty strong, well-built club athletes, some of them
rubber-shod, with short coats buttoned close around their
shapely chests, climbed on the stage of Wallack's Theater
last night and labored like blacksmiths for an hour to either
tire out or expose Lulu Hurst, the phenomenon of the
nineteenth century. About one hundred more athletes were
there also to take part and watch the fun.   The athletes retired from the stage after the performance covered with
perspiration and confusion.   The Georgia girl, who had
tossed them about like so many jackstraws, was perfectly
cool and not in the least tired.   She seemed to be in better
condition and capable of greater demonstration at the close
of the performance than at the beginning of it.   Men and
women were pushing one another for standing room
throughout the house.   Persons who had been at the performance every night for a week were there again.   There
were plenty of notable faces in the audience.   Ex-Senator
Roscoe Conkling watched every movement the girl made
very closely.   John T. Raymond got off in a corner where
he thought he could get a closer view and saw the same
thing over again.   General Dan Sickles was in a front seat.
The Rev. Dr. Hepworth laughed heartily at the antics of
the club men.   Joseph F. Loubat chatted with some of the
7 1

ladies in one of the boxes. More women were present than on any previous night. * * * * *

"The club men poured on the stage the moment the invitation was given. They worked together and determined to produce a sensational 'exposè' if they could. The first young man braced himself to the floor and grasped a billiard cue as though he would c-r-u-s-h it in his fingers. He was pushed unceremoniously against the scene and sat down. * * * * * * * *

" A tall, slender youth with a tuberose was greeted with cries of 'good-evening.' He proved a good stayer, but was vanquished like all the others. A stout Englishman thought he was safe if he did not look the girl in the eyes. He closed his own trusting lids and remained firm. The Phenomenon laughed, the Englishman looked up, and lo! he was gone. The biggest athlete of all grasped the cue. 'Now,' said Mr. Atkinson, 'he is going to push it to the floor.' He did nothing of the kind. He pranced around for awhile like a Shetland pony, and fell all in a heap at the footlights. Two, and then three men grasped the cue, and it was snapped like a reed in their hands. * * *

"A strong chair was produced. A paymaster in the army grasped it and held it out straight from the chest. The 'Phenomenon' simply laid the palm of her hand on the seat, and he wiggled around like an eel.

"Major Benjamin Franklin Pond tried it again, and he also moved around pretty lively. Miss Hurst placed her hands over his and bore the chair to the floor, the Major doing his best to hold it up.

" 'Now,' said Mr. Atkinson, 'I should like the gentleman to tell the audience whether he felt the pressure of

Miss Hurst's hands'? The major advanced to the foot-lights, and said:

"'I felt a very *delicate* pressure of the lady's hands.'

*   *   *   *   *   *   *   *   *

"For the next fifteen minutes the club athletes did some pretty hard work. The sweat rolled down in streams from their foreheads, as they bore down three at a time on a chair, and this young girl, without any apparent muscular exertion, would not let them put it on the floor. The 'Phenomenon' simply laughed at them. She can't help laughing. Every time she tries to control her laugh and look sober, she looks unnatural. It is not a boisterous, hearty laugh, but a low, rippling chuckle. The 'Phenomenon' has a very peculiar habit of running her hands through her hair, after the fashion of an excitable platform orator. She is not a tricky, scheming looking girl and does not look anything like smart enough to attempt to impose on a New York audience. The manager and the Wonder certainly allow the curious skeptics to make all the investigations they desire to. An intensely amusing feature accompanied all the tests. At frequent intervals when the Force seemed to delay its coming for a moment, it was observed that Miss Hurst's merry laugh was the prelude to its onslaught on the waiting victim. The audience observed this, and soon the cry was heard all over the house when a fresh victim stood up before the 'Power,' 'Smile on him, Lulu! Smile on him!' and when the laugh came the victim went.   *   *   *   *   *

"A man weighing nearly three hundred pounds dropped into the chair and the 'Phenomenon' lifted him as though he were a child. The great audience grew more and more interested and pushed further front. At one time fully fifty people pushed their way on the stage and kept their eyes on the girl's hands and feet. One man clasped her fore-arm as she lifted a fellow much heavier than himself from the floor. He vowed she did not move a muscle of that arm. Nearly every man on the stage had a different opinion and none were slow in expressing themselves. Some said it was superior muscular power, but if so the exhibition was the more remarkable. Without any apparent effort the 'Phenomenon' twitched about, as a cat would a mouse, three men who boast of their strength in the gymnasium. They struggled manfully, but she threw them in a heap. One man burned his light trousers in the footlights and every one laughed at him. Suddenly a young man stepped to the front, and shouted:

" 'Say, these fellows have rubber on their shoes and in their hands. It ain't fair.' No one paid any attention to him. The 'Phenomenon' whisked 200 pounds avoirdupois around on a billiard cue and threw the whole scene into confusion."

The New York *Tribune*, in a long account, says:

. . . . " When the curtain again rose two huge men walked up the red-carpeted steps amid roars of applause. They were Maj. Pond and Prof. Lafflin, the athlete, both of them good men and weighing an unknown quantity. Prof. Lafflin tried various tests but was forced to give in every time. He tried the billiard cue test over again, carefully wiping it with his handkerchief before grasping it. He tried the chair test and reeled about the stage. . . . . The spectators laughed when Miss Hurst dragged these men about the stage as they clung convulsively to the rungs of a chair; they shrieked as a young man in a green coat stepped confidently up the steps, seized the chair, and, amid a wild endeavor to force it to the ground, tumbled ingloriously under it; they roared as the aged man first experimented upon wiped his brow wearily after another trial and walked off the stage out of the house. Finally, when, by placing her hands at each side of the chair, Miss Hurst made it twist about as though imbued with life, they applauded as even Lester Wallack would find it difficult to make them applaud with all his art and genius."

These are only a few of the accounts written about my early performances in the city. The entire city press devoted columns daily to giving accounts of the "Wonder." The opposition to me of such men as Dr. Forrest and their charges of fraud, etc., only seemed to add fuel to the fire. The papers all took my part and the people all tried to get to our performances. To my mind one of the most remarkable things connected with our exhibitions in the great city was the constant, universal, unsolicited, enthusiastic endorsement and support of my entertainments there by the great New York City press.

A special from New York, at this time, to the Savannah *Morning News*, dated July 10th, says among other things in an extensive write-up, headed as follows:

"OPINIONS DIVIDED AS TO HER POWERS.

"*Gossip in the Metropolis—Correspondence of The Morning News.*

"New York, July 10th—Miss Hurst, the Georgia Wonder, is just now the talk of the town. People are divided in their opinions as to her capabilities, but even those who think that there is some trick in her performances do not really know what to make of them.   *   *   *

"It is only the people who have seen her, but have not experienced her powers, who profess to deride them. Those who have been whirled about at the option of Miss Hurst, despite their utmost resistance, think, if they do not acknowledge it, as Mr. Grant, of the Union Club, did last evening, that her performances, if she merely uses her muscle, *are more wonderful than if she possessed some secret force.* Police Captain Williams has been converted to the secret force theory without experiencing Miss Hurst's powers. He earnestly desired to try a bout with her, but he wisely concluded that a captain of police would lose in dignity if a promiscuous audience saw him mastered by a young girl. He has felt her arms, however, and says she has no muscle with which to perform her feats of apparent strength. Dr. Forrest, who openly denounced Miss Hurst as a 'transparent fraud,' on Tuesday night, is a physician of no reputation, whose opinion has no professional weight.

"That Miss Hurst's performances are considered very extraordinary is shown by the space they occupy in the different newspapers. The *Sun* this morning, in spite of its page report of the Chicago Convention, devotes nearly a column and a half to a description of Miss Hurst and her seance at Wallack's last night. In short, the general opinion regarding Miss Hurst may be summed up in the expression that there are more things in heaven and earth than are dreamed of in the philosophy of most men."

CHAPTER XIII.

THE "GREAT UNKNOWN" AND THE "JERSEY LILY."

A Complimentary "to the Players"—The Falling of the "Stars"—" The Superstition of the People Depressing to Me."

A request numerously signed had been presented to our manager asking a special exhibition for the benefit of the "Profession."

On account of their engagements taking place in other theaters at the same hour as ours at Wallack's, they had not been able to see my performance. In order to accommodate them we decided to give them a complimentary matinee performance at Madison Square Theater. All the star actors of the city were present, and many who were not stars. The theater was well filled. Before the performance was over the "stars" fell as they had not done since the great "falling" of 1834, which the old people tell us about.

Among the large number of ladies present, I can recall Miss Georgia Cayvan and her sister Alice, Mrs. Louisa Eldridge of the Madison Square Company, known to the profession as "Aunty Louise," pretty Mattie Ferguson, Theresa Johnson of "Our Boarding House," Kate Mor-

ris, Bertha Welby, Kate Castleton, Pauline Hall, Emma
Carson, May Barrington, Emma Schultz, Kate Rice,
Marion Russell, and Mrs. Langtry, the "Jersey Lily."
I do not know that I could give a better account of this
performance than to quote the one given in the *New York
Star*, which was headed as follows:

"MISS LULU AND THE LILY.

"*An Extraordinary Exhibition of the Georgia Wonder's
Power—Mrs. Langtry Turns a Somersault—Billy Ed-
wards Knocked Out in One Round—Scientists at Sea—
The Problem Still Unsolved.*

" The Georgia wonder still continues to excite wonderment. Her remarkable exhibition of psychic force, or
whatever the agency may be, by which she exercises her
mysterious power, reduces Dr. Home's seances almost to
the level of the commonplace by comparison. There cannot be any doubt of the genuineness of her singular feats
of strength. That she is unaided is beyond dispute.

" The reply, therefore, of the doorkeeper of the Madison Square Theater to the *Star* reporter yesterday afternoon was perfectly natural:

" ' Miss Hurst? of course you want to see Miss Hurst;
everybody does. Go right inside,'—and the attendant assumed a perfectly-proper-I-am-not-surprised expression
that was full of conviction, metaphorically speaking, that
Miss Hurst was in everybody's mouth.

" Much amused at the man's self-convincing manner,
the reporter entered the theater and took his seat among
the audience in absolute ignorance of what was in store.
It was a performance for the theatrical profession, and the

'stars' and lesser lights were out in superabundance. Among others of the famous lights present was the renowned and beautiful Mrs. Langtry, the 'Jersey Lily.'

"It was known how she boasted of her physical prowess, and had said that she rode and hunted with her brother, and had a thoroughly developed muscular system. She had expressed a great desire to test the boasted power of the Georgia Wonder.

"In the comedy that ensued on the stage Mrs. Langtry and the Georgia Wonder were the leading characters. It was a comedy in one act—a comedy, too, that had not been rehearsed, and there were no 'waits.' The Jersey Lily had heard of Miss Lulu Hurst and wanted to know her. Before the acquaintance had terminated, Mrs. Langtry had arrived at the conclusion that to know Miss Lulu was equivalent to a life's memory. It would scarcely be fair to the Wonder to say that Mrs. Langtry was prejudiced, but at any rate she was shocked before the performance was over. And judging by the developments, it was a pretty strong shock, too.

"A flutter of excitement ran through the audience when the wish of the dainty English woman was made known. Mrs. Langtry rose gracefully in her seat and made her way to the stage. Miss Hurst passed her fingers quickly through her bangs. As the Lily tripped on the stage the Wonder laughed and looked her victim steadily in the face.

"'Mrs. Langtry will hold the billiard cue and try to stand still,' said the manager.

Mrs. Langtry looked nervous, but she took the cue. So far it was quite professional. The audience tittered, the

Wonder laughed—a sure sign that she meant business.
The Lily's white hands grasped the cue and the Wonder
placed one of her palms upon it. In the twinkling of an
eye the Lily began to oscillate. She swayed to and fro,
then' she braced herself for a final effort. The Wonder
caught the Lily's eye and the actress was gone. With a
bound Mrs. Langtry was flung into the air, and turning a
somersault, she was pitched against a scene and went tum-
bling down the stage steps. It was not a stage fall by
any manner of means, although it was a fall off the stage.
The excitement was immense, utterly beyond all bounds of
control, and the attention of the audience was divided
between applause for the Wonder and apprehension for the
Lily's safety. A dozen gallants went to her assistance,
and when the English beauty got her breath, she looked
around in amazement and asked, " what had struck her? "
She rushed into the private office and began to tell a tale
which moved the hearts of the managers to pity.

" ' Why, it's wonderful,' said she. ' I don't know what
has happened. It was like a flash of lightning followed
by a thunderbolt. It's a mercy I'm alive; I don't want
any more of it. I have had a great curiosity to test this
power, but I am now fully satisfied. It is indeed the
most wonderful thing I ever saw.'

" Mrs. Langtry's elegant dress was badly rumpled and
torn, and she sustained several bruises.

"Then 'Aunt Louisa' tried it, begging the Power to be
mild, but she suffered such a shock that for a few minutes
her tongue was paralyzed. This was thought to be a phenomenon.

"Billy Edwards also took the stage, and was knocked

out in one round, much to the amusement of the audience. Ed. Gilmore, Robert Fraser, Bartley Campbell, and Drs. Carnochan and Kissam also had several bouts with the Wonder, and came off second best. The medical men said they felt a strange power, but no muscular force. Five ladies went upon the stage, and failed to put the chair to the floor while the Wonder's hand was upon it.

"The Wonder next tried conclusions with a fat man in spectacles, who was trying to stand still and hold a chair, but was interrupted by the current from the Wonder's fingers. This was Dr. Pippo. The fat doctor bobbed about frantically, and finally landed face downward, to the great amusement of the audience. * * * * *

"Men of Falstaffian proportions like Major Pond and Lysander Thompson; others of Herculean strength like Lafflin the athlete; Ettlinger, the caterer, whose muscles are like iron, and vigorous, sinewy fellows like Dr. Forest and Harry Hill, are all vanquished in a few moments and sent spinning round the stage like so many babies.

"The umbrella feat created immense amusement. Of course, it's easy to hold an umbrella still; they think so, and the unsuspecting man grasps it. The Wonder puts her fingers on the handle, and the umbrella flops over the victim's head and wriggles like a mad thing. Then the three scoot over the stage, dodging in and out of the wings until somebody's face is bruised, or a number of spectators are placed *hors de combat*. * * * * * * *

"The chair feat is the *piece de resistance* of all. Often six strong men are unable to force the chair to the floor while the Wonder's hands rest lightly upon it; and again fat men, weighing sometimes two hundred and fifty pounds, sitting in the chair, are violently thrown out by the Wonder placing her open palm against the posts of the chair.

"Dr. E. B. Foote, Jr., a young, vigorous man, was whirled around with lightning rapidity. 'What do I think of it?' said he, as he gasped for breath. 'It's wonderful! She could have thrown me anywhere. I don't know whether it's electric, muscular, or satanic force. I had no time to think. I shouldn't have been alive now if I hadn't got away!'

"Mr. Fred Braisted, a well known athlete, weighing two hundred pounds, declared that it was not muscular force. 'Why, I could lay out four men her weight, and not exert myself. I put out all my strength, and yet she regularly scattered me!'

"Harry Hill was again worsted, and jumped from the stage in mad haste, crying: 'Let's have a beer, boys! That Wonder's a terror. Strength! Hit haint no strength. Why, I could a housted her hif she hadn't a put hon the power. Where the —— she gits hit from, Hi don't know, now blest hif Hi do. Hi suppose hits electricity, but where does she keep hit? that's what Hi should like to find hout.'

"'That's just what I say!' chimed in a venerable-looking individual. 'I say it's electricity, and she's got it stored in her boots!'

"At this the crowd roared.

"Louis Ettlinger, of No. 49 East Ninth street, said: 'My muscles are all strained and sore after my bout with her, and yet I'm a strong, heavy man, and possess great physical power. She doesn't exercise her muscles. At one time I felt a thrill go through me and I lost all power of resistance. Dr. Forest's cry of muscular force is absurd!'

Dr. Henry A. Mott, who weighs one hundred

and ninety-six pounds, was sprawled around all over the floor with ease. Said he: ' I should like to experiment with this girl with the dynamometer before I give an opinion. But, seriously, I do not think she is abnormally strong. There is no muscular force used so far as I can see.' Public opinion is simply dazed at the Wonder, and the doctors are all at sea. The spiritualists are complaisant and wear a satisfied, know-all look. Ex-Editor O. B. Silkman, the gentleman with the Nepoleonic face, tried conclusions with the Wonder and was all knocked out. His antics caused the audience immense fun. In answer to the cries of speech, speech, he said: ' I fully believe in the phenomenon, and think it's due to spirits.' This is the view all the spiritualists take of it, but it is said the Wonder and her parents vigorously denounce the spirit theory, and are violently opposed to all such superstitious notions."

I have quoted about half of this article, which was illustrated all the way through with cuts of the different tests, to give an idea of the lengthy and elaborate writeups the press gave my performances. This is but a sample. All of the dailies and illustrated journals gave repeated and elaborate accounts all the while I was in New York.

There was one thing that always annoyed me, and that was to know that so many people harbored such superstitious ideas about my "Power," and classed it as due to "spirits." This weighed upon me more than anything else, and made me ask myself often if my performances were not assuming proportions, to accomplish an amount of harm vastly more than I could manage to counteract. As young as I was I hated to see such ideas gaining ground and finding reinforcements through and by means of my phenomena.

CHAPTER XIV.

MATINÉE TO LADIES ONLY.

They Meet the "Great Unknown" Face to Face in the Amphitheater at Wallack's—Nym Crinkle Philosophizes Concerning "The Power"—New York Still Overwhelmed in Mystery.

After our special entertainment to theatrical people and after the papers of the city had given full accounts of Mrs. Langtry's experience with the "Wonderful Power," then the requests began to pour in for a matinee for "ladies only." These requests were so urgent and numerous that we were forced to accede to them. So on Wednesday, July 15th, the following notice was to be seen on the bulletin board at Wallack's:

"Matinee, 2:30. To Ladies Only. Lulu Hurst—The Wonder of the 19th Century."

The hour for the exhibition arrived. The house was packed from pit to dome. All the ushers were then excluded, and no one was admitted except ladies. I never had an audience to be in more perfect sympathy with the "Power"; almost every one seemed to believe thoroughly in the "Great Unknown." If a skeptic showed her head she was greeted with a storm of hisses. In the New York

World's account of this performance I find these lines on this point :

" After the demolition of the several ladies who had come on the stage the audience would call for speech! speech! but the call was seldom responded to. The first to answer it was a slim woman in black and white check dress, whose black eyes flashed fire. She had been trying to push the chair to the floor, and declared the Wonder had hold of the rounds when she was only supposed to have her palms resting against them. The audience took this bit of skepticism coldly. In fact, skepticism was not tolerated for a moment. The instant an incredulous, muscular woman seriously contested the Wonder's powers, she was hissed from the stage."

I enjoyed my performance for " ladies only" very much. It was novel and very amusing to me, for my tests were almost always with big, strong men, ladies not coming to take part before mixed audiences. I am glad to say that my own sex stood the fire of the " Great Unknown " just as well as the men. They were not one bit more nervous and excited than men. The Power appeared more gallant with them than with men, however, and seemed to handle them more tenderly.

After our exhibition to ladies had proved such a big success our party was the recipient of numerous invitations to private homes. Large offers were made us for private exhibitions, but we accepted none. Our receipts had reached such proportions that money had gotten to be not much of an object to us, and as private exhibitions were in a measure distasteful to us, we avoided them as much as possible.

I think I can safely say our performance was the best advertised affair ever put before the public, and the pleasurable part of it was the advertising was all gratuitous, and this is the best kind of advertising. Every paper, great and small, seemed to be my friend, and all were warm and enthusiastic champions of the " Great Unknown."

My management wrote no advertising articles, and paid for none. I want to take occasion now, even at this late day, to express my unbounded gratitude for this journalistic munificence and magnanimity.

We exhibited in New York twenty-four nights and never had a poor audience. On the day of my last performance, even the ticket-seller at Wallack's, who had been in service for years, showed himself a friend, champion, and admirer of the "Power." He said he had grown tired of everything in the way of a performance of any kind, but his interest in the " Power " was so great and his curiosity so overpowering, that he would employ a substitute to take his place at the office after the entertainment began, and come in the theater to see the "Wonder." He said to me when I went to leave: " Miss Lulu, I hate to see you go. Your exhibition is the only one I have had the slightest curiosity to see in ten years. But I must say I have been intensely interested in yours, and I heartily wish you the same success elsewhere that you have met with in New York." His kind words linger with me yet.

I will close my account of my New York performances by giving two quotations from the New York papers. The first from the New York *Truth:*

"ECHOES FROM THE FOYER—MISS LULU HURST NOT A FRAUD.

" The slight breeze of excitement caused by John A.

McCaull's attack upon Mr. Rudolph Aronson has been entirely lost in the storm which Lulu Hurst has raised and is still raising at Wallack's Theater, and New York seems to be literally fermenting in its anxiety to determine the character and the causes of the peculiar force which this young girl possesses, and not a few of our citizens have rendered themselves ridiculous in their efforts to unravel the mystery. More than this, the community is becoming rapidly divided into two classes, one of which adheres to the idea that Miss Hurst is enabled to perform her remarkable feats by the assistance of some inexplicable magnetic or nervous force, while the other truculently advances the theory that everything the young lady does is due to simple muscular power. Whenever a party of the first class meets a party of the second class, the Georgia Wonder at once becomes the theme of discussion, and logic and science both become exhausted in the ensuing struggle without any apparent result.

"So far as I am individually concerned, I am free to admit my inability to explain Miss Hurst's power. I have tested the umbrella, the billiard cue, and the chair feats, and the fact that the force she exerts is so much greater than that which I have heretofore encountered in either woman or man, leads me to incline to the magnetic theory, or at least to the existence of a force more potent than that of mere muscular power. But this is the question for scientists to determine, and I shall not bother my brain with it. I may say, however, that if we are to explain Miss Hurst's power on the muscular theory, she becomes a *greater wonder than ever !*

" With regard to the cry of fraud which has been raised

against Miss Hurst, it seems to me to be most unfounded. When she came before the New York public, the management announced that she would do some remarkable things, but ventured no explanation of the causes leading to such results. On the contrary, it was explicitly stated that neither Miss Hurst nor any one connected with her understood the force or power she possessed.

"Where, then, does the fraud come in? Miss Hurst has done what she claimed to do, and has left the question of cause to the public to settle. She did not say that she threw strong men down by magnetism, nor that she lifted Hubert O. Thompson by muscular force. She simply did these things, and I doubt whether she has ever attempted to solve the problem as to how she did them. Miss Hurst may not be possessed with the slightest magnetism, and may accomplish all her feats by unusual clever application of remarkable muscular force; but is that any reason for calling her a fraud? In all justice, I think not. * * *

"But the arguments *pro* and *con* upon this subject serve only to advertise the Power, and in the meantime she goes on shoving big, strong men about, and fagging them out, apparently without the slightest exertion or the least fatigue.

"Yesterday afternoon, the audience was composed largely of ladies, many of whom went upon the stage and tested the "Force" to their entire satisfaction. It was the first time in New York that her own sex had experimented with her, and Miss Hurst seemed greatly delighted.

"Among others struggling with the Wonder yesterday, was Mr. Joseph Murphy, the actor, who has an abiding faith in his own strength, and who therefore mounted the stage with the greatest assurance. The consequence was that he fared worse than usual, for after a few minutes' struggling, he was thrown flat on his back.

" ' Well '? I said to him as he came flushed, puffing and perspiring off the stage.

" ' I don't know what it is," he answered, "but I'd rather try to hold a wild horse than that girl! ' "

* * * *

The next and last quotation I will give is from a long article written by that famous literateur, Nym Crinkle, in the New York *World:*

" Will she be sooner or later understood ? Here is a manifestation of some kind of energy that does not betray the usual physical symptoms of muscular power. A girl, whose *flexor longis* and *flexor brevis* are as soft as a corn-starch pudding, stands before a thousand people, and three or four of the strongest men in the assemblage are asked to match their combined physical strength against her energy, and she invariably overcomes them. They strain and perspire. Their intense muscular contraction betrays itself in their limbs and distended breasts. They grow red in the face and pant. Their hearts beat rapidly, and there stands the laughing girl unperturbed. Her pulse is unchanged, so is her respiration, except when, in order to keep a contact with the struggling men, she is compelled to move rapidly after them.

" At the conclusion of the experiment these men shake their heads sagaciously. They get down on their knees to look for traps and wires, and arrive at the conclusion that Miss Hurst is simply the most muscular girl they have ever met, or the cleverest trickster.

" I suppose if you were to take that Wallack audience
as a base, and put Dr. Hammond on top as the apex, you
would have such a Gizeh of granitic and incorrigible
prejudice as could not be found anywhere.

"The only difference between the audience and the
doctor is that one is willing to investigate if it can be entertained, and the other isn't unless he can prove it a
fraud.

" Both are much more anxious to have it proved that
Miss Hurst is stronger than six of the strongest men in
New York, than to acknowledge that she is the innocent
medium of some yet unformulated energy of whose nature
she is entirely ignorant, and over which she has no voli-
tional control."

CHAPTER XV.

THE POWER IN THE "HUB"—THE CHALLENGE TO JOHN L. SULLIVAN.

The "Great Unknown" Deserts Me, and for the First and Only Time Leaves Me Forceless, Powerless and Helpless— A Moment Fraught with Momentous Consequences to Us— The Punishment of the Terror-stricken Skeptic.

From New York we hurried on to Boston, where we found that our fame had preceded us. We opened our engagement at the Globe Theater, one of the handsomest theatrical buildings in the United States. We entered the "Hub" with a feeling of considerable curiosity as to how the peculiar, ultra Boston learning would view the "Power." Our audiences were all that we could desire, and the large theatre was packed at every performance. The success of the "Unknown" in carrying everything before it was as complete as at any place we ever exhibited. It showed no respect for Boston *cultuah,* nor the historic memories of Bunker Hill; nor was it awed by the sanctified shades of Emerson and Longfellow; nor did the wild, unsubdued element of the "Great Unknown" show reverence for the home of the great Franklin, who first discovered and

chained the untutored, fiery fluid of the clouds and en-
slaved it to the perpetual service of man.

The Boston *Transcript*, in a lengthy account, says:

"THE GEORGIA WHAT—IS—IT?"

"Miss Lulu Hurst, the Georgia Wonder, made her first
appearance in Boston at the Globe Theater last evening,
before a crowded house; not only the seats, but the standing room occupied.   The audience was a complex and a
comprehensive one, containing representatives from almost
every social plane.   Many visited the theater in a spirit of
scientific investigation, and many through curiosity and
fun.   There was plenty of fun and enough of the marvellous to feed, if not to satisfy, one's curiosity.   A number
of gentlemen, well known in the city, formed the committee in the several tests of Miss Hurst's unexplained
power.   *   *   *   *   *   *   *   *

"Those who expressed an opinion to the audience after
testing the power, pronounced it wonderful and unexplainable.   *   *   *   *   *   *   *   *   *

"She hurled heavy weights about the stage quite as
easily as she did the lighter weights.   *   *   *   *

"One scientific gentleman, after one trial, wrapped his
hands in silk handkerchiefs, but notwithstanding these non-
conductors, he was conducted to the floor in double-quick
time.   *   *   *   *   *   *   *   *

"The performance closed with the united attempt of six
strong men, including the heavy Mr. Dempster, who could
not have weighed less than two hundred and fifty pounds,
and Mr. J. Boyle O'Reilly, to force to the floor a chair
upon which the Wonder rested her hand; but they did
not succeed.   *   *   *   *   *   *   *

"The young lady's performances are marvelous, whether they proceed from muscularity, psychic force, magnetism or trickery; and whatever may be her secret power, she is well worth investigating by everybody."

Another of the Boston dailies says:

"Miss Hurst undoubtedly showed some wonderful power which could scarcely have been muscular, for there is no man in Boston, including Jno. L. Sullivan, who could by simple exertion of strength, hold up a chair with one hand against the united efforts of four heavy men, one of whom did not weigh less than two hundred and fifty pounds."

While in Boston we were anxious to pit "The Great Unknown" against the renowned Jno. L. Sullivan. The challenge was really given as an advertisement, for we had no doubt that he would go down in utter defeat before "the Unknown."

John L. Sullivan was, at that time, the "Pride of Boston," and the champion Goliath of the world. He had not then met his "David" in "Gentleman Jim," but stalked the earth the undisputable champion of the world. But I knew, in fact, he was no stronger, if as strong, as the wonderful athlete, Professor Lafflin, whom I met and vanquished in New York. But his reputation was greater, hence my desire to pit "The Great Unknown" against him. The papers of Boston announced the challenge in great shape; but Sullivan was too smart to fall into the trap set for him. He declared that however great his physical power might be, he was not going to pit his strength and skill against a *Supernatural Power*, and we could not get him into the tests.

Without attempting to give detailed accounts of my

various entertainments in Boston, I will pass on and give an experience we had at a matinée for "ladies only." I mention this performance because it was the only time in the history of the "Power" that it ever failed to assert itself.

It came about in this way:

At this matinée no gentlemen were allowed, even the ushers being excluded. The entertainment had progressed finely, the Power vanquishing the ladies without mercy or gallantry, and was about half over, when a lady in the rear of the house rose up and asked of Mr. Atkinson, my manager, if he had not advertised for a matinée for ladies only. He told her that he had, and that he was not aware that there were any gentlemen in the house, and also suggested that if there were any present we would be glad to have them withdraw. Whereupon she said:

"Well, Mr. Manager, I do not mean to say that there are any gentlemen in the audience, but you are present and we want you to withdraw, because we think that you mesmerize Miss Hurst and make her do these wonderful things."

My manager replied:

"To convince you that you are in error, I have only to state that Miss Hurst gave exhibitions several weeks before I ever saw her."

She said:

"Yes, sir, I can understand how easy it is to make a statement, but I also know that it is sometimes difficult to prove it."

In other words, she rather suggested that my manager had falsified. Her remark was wholly uncalled for, and

was very cutting and unkind, and the audience hissed her
for it. My manager told her that it would be impossible
for him to leave the stage, as it was necessary to have
some one present to introduce the different tests, and to
explain to the audience what each test consisted of.

He then continued the entertainment by inviting some
lady on the stage to make a test. When I went to make
the test, the "Power" had apparently deserted me; it would
do nothing. I put my hands on the chair, and the "Great
Unknown" had vanished. We then tried the cane and umbrella, but all to no purpose. I could do nothing. My manager, to relieve the embarrassment, called on the orchestra,
and we went into the green room. My parents, who
were there, were informed that the "Power" had gone from
me, and they were amazed! We sat down and discussed
the situation, which was alarming. Here was a big audience waiting for the wonders of the "Unknown," and "It"
gone from me, leaving me powerless and helpless. This
terrible contingency—the loss of my Power, which we had
all dreaded, and which we had been warned by physicians
might happen, now seemed a dreadful reality. The
"Power" seemed to have passed away in an instant upon
the excitement caused by the skeptical lady's attack on my
manager. The impending question now was, would it return, or was it gone forever? We made different tests in
almost breathless despair but the "Unknown" came not.
What could we do? We must do something and that
quickly, for the audience would not be patient indefinitely.
After a little while, my father said:

"Lulu, try this chair."

I put my hand on it and—*no Power.* My manager, after

a few moments more, took the chair. I placed my hands on it, and in a little while *he was on his head.* Our joy knew no bounds! I realized that the "Unknown" was with me again. I was glad, and *I was mad* that we should have gone through such a fearful strain, all on account of the discourteous woman. After my manager got up from the floor, I said:

"Yes, and that's the way I am going to do that woman, and when I go out there I want you to insist upon her coming to the stage!"

When we returned to the stage, and the exhibition had progressed a while longer to our perfect satisfaction, my manager stated to the audience that in order to satisfy some in the house who seemed to doubt his statements, and who desired that he withdraw from the stage, that he had decided to do so on one condition, viz.: that the incredulous lady herself come upon the stage and undergo the test.

She refused to do so at first, but the audience insisted so earnestly that she finally had to yield and come up. My manager then withdrew to the wings and there watched, as he afterwards told me, with breathless anxiety, the result. I will quote his words as to what took place:

"It seemed an age to me before the 'Power' came, but heavens! when it did come it was like a cyclone. It took that skeptical, curt lady up one side of the big stage and then down the other with the speed of a race-horse, and the power of an enraged tigress. It then rushed her to the rear, carrying dismay and disorder into the ranks of the other investigators. It then hurled her back toward the front. Every woman in the house was now standing up, yelling and screaming at the top of their voices. On they came, the woman and the "Great Unknown" right on towards the footlights! The now terror-stricken woman was screaming at the top of her voice, 'Help! help! help!' but the 'Power' heeded not her distress nor her cry, but forced her on with tremendous speed to the footlights! The audience now realized her great danger, as they saw she was coming over the footlights into the orchestra. I had watched the entire performance from the wings, and took in the dangerous situation, and rushed out just in time to catch her around the waist and prevent her from being hurled down into the orchestra. I then said to her: 'I now hope, madam, you can understand why it is necessary for a man to be on the stage.' "

*　　*　　*　　*　　*　　*　　*　　*　　*

It might be amusing to some of my readers and instructive to others, to quote the following sample of Boston poetry which made its appearance in one of the papers of the Hub while I was there, headed

"AT THE GLOBE."

" Lulu Hurst, the Georgia Wonder,
　　Now is all the rage;
Oh, but it's a treat to see her
　　Yank 'em round the stage!

" First it was a bad umbrella
　　Twisted nside out,
While the man, who held the handle,
　　Whirled around about.

" When she did the same thing over
　　With a stick or cane;
Athletes in her hands were playthings,
　　All their muscles vain.

" Light or heavy, what the difference?
   Blown about like chaff;
'Dempster' weighing pounds three hundred,
   'Connally' about half.

" Oh, the mild and stormy Lulu
   How she made 'em stare!
Four athletic lumps of fellows
   Couldn't hold a chair.

" To explain the magic maiden
   Useless all harangues;
Is the power within her elbows
   Or within her bangs?

" Or, perhaps her eyes so wondrous,
   Luminous and bright,
Which she turned on every subject
   Like a summer night?

" One thing though, is very certain,
   Settled beyond doubt,
Elbows, eyes, or bangs, or something,
   Seemed to knock 'em out!"

CHAPTER XVI.

THE "POWER" IN PROVIDENCE.

The "Power" and the Pleasure Seekers of Saratoga—The Dilemma at Newport—My Father and Manager to the Rescue at a Critical Moment.

After our failure to get Mr. John L. Sullivan into the contest with what he deemed the "Supernatural Power" of a fourteen year old girl, and after we had come so near losing this power following the discourteous remarks of a lady, there was nothing of unusual interest occurred during our ten days' engagement in Boston.

The usual crowds and excitement attended us in this cultured city, and they were just as much amazed and mystified as the audiences in other cities, who laid no stress on their superior intelligence or. culture. Chaperoned by charming friends, it was our pleasure to visit the many historic points in and about Boston, and we left this splendid city "fully persuaded" that it contained more of an historic nature than any city on the continent.

From Boston we went to Providence, R. I. Here we gave several exhibitions to crowded houses and intensely excited audiences. The press here had a great deal to say about " The Georgia Wonder " and her marvelous power.

The *Telegram* says among other things in a column and a half article :

" That the young lady has created quite a furor is beyond question, as her exhibitions in New York and Boston have been attended night after night by large audiences, and although every effort has been made to discover some trick, or some reason to account for the mysterious power by which she mastered strong men, thus far all such efforts have been unavailing.   *   *   *   *   *

" The party invited upon the stage evidently had read the reports of the manner in which the Wonder had mopped up the floor with powerful athletes in New York, and were rather backward in coming forward to assist in the tests. Manager Hackett finally came and the tests commenced. He grasped a chair firmly, holding it about breast high, and then Miss Hürst placed the palms of her hands on the side and back, and soon the well-built manager of the opera house began to sway to and fro and was very red in the face, while the young lady, without any apparent effort, rushed him around the stage despite all his efforts to resist her, and he finally gave it up, looking as if he had just tackled the Jap wrestler, while the Wonder looked as unruffled as if she had been merely trying on a new spring bonnet."   Then follows a description of a number of other tests with the committee, and the article continues :

"The last test and most remarkable was with the billiard cue. The cue was placed horizontally across the palm of Miss Hurst's hand and without her having any hold upon it at all. A gentleman then grasped it with both hands, and tried to force it across the palm of her open hand to the floor, but, although he was an unusually strong man, he could not, with all his strength, accomplish the task, and gave it up.

"The fact has been stated by some of the strong men Miss Hurst has encountered, that she is merely a very powerful and muscular girl, but that does not seem possible, for she has no development of muscle in her arms to account for the strength by which she was enabled to overcome a man like the athlete Lafflin, of New York.

"Every one was satisfied that the power, whatever it may be, natural or unnatural, was a mystery to them, and that the Wonder accomplished everything that is claimed for her."

The Providence *Journal* gave a number of accounts in detail of the various tests at the performances, and says:

"Altogether, they are wonderful and curious and excited no little interest. None could explain the source of this power, but the general impression among those who witnessed the various experiments was that at least the power did not come from muscular force."

The following is a description from the same *Journal* of the appearance of the "Georgia Wonder":

"Miss Lulu was introduced and naturally attracted much attention. She acknowledged the introduction by a bow which, though not the personification of grace, was far from awkward, and indicated her confidence to accomplish the task which she was about to attempt. She is a tall, well-formed young lady, unusually well developed for her age, fifteen years, with shapely arms and hands, but giving no indication of special muscular development. Her face

is oval and full, with a ruddy glow upon the cheeks;
her eyes are dark and clear, while the lips show a tendency to droop; dark hair, almost black indeed, cut
short in front, falls over and half conceals the forehead,
while at the sides and back it hangs in wavy ringlets.
Her face in repose would be taken for that of a light-
hearted schoolgirl, while the ever ready smile which
plays over it could not fail to impress one with the idea
that the young woman is a particularly good-humored
and pleasant person."

From Providence we went to Troy, Albany, Fall River
and a number of other cities, where our exhibitions were
always received with the same enthusiasm and wonderment as had characterized them everywhere.

After our engagement at Albany we took a ten days'
rest and went to Saratoga Springs. It was in the midst of
the gaiety season and the hotels were all crowded. We
managed to get apartments at the Grand Union Hotel,
and it was no sooner known that "The Georgia Wonder" was at the hotel than the requests for interviews,
etc., began to pour in. Then came the request for an
exhibition, but there was no suitable house in the town
to hold the crowd, so it was arranged to have the exhibition in the large skating rink, "The Casino." This
would hold some two thousand people. A temporary,
though strong, stage was built with ropes running around
it, to keep the victims of the "Great Unknown" from
being thrown off. When the performance took place
the house was filled, and a more enthusiastic audience
we never had. Here we gave three exhibitions and spent
a delightful week.

The Saratoga *Evening Journal* says:

"About one thousand two hundred ladies and gentlemen assembled at the Casino last Saturday evening to witness the performance given by Miss Lulu Hurst, "The Georgia Wonder." The phenomenal force exhibited by this young lady was certainly remarkable and could not be explained. She does not understand the nature of the power that is directed by her will. It exists, and that is all the explanation made.   *   *.   *   *   *

"At no time during the wonderful performance did she appear to exert any physical strength."

The success of the Saratoga engagements, so hurriedly gotten up, was so great that the requests came from Newport and Long Branch for exhibitions there. The date was fixed and we went first to Newport. Here was one of the most fashionable audiences we ever appeared before, and probably an audience that represented greater wealth than any single audience we ever faced, for Newport, unlike Saratoga and Long Branch, is the resort of the wealthy, aristocratic class alone.

Our boat was due to arrive at 7 P.M., but unfortunately was nearly two hours late, and before we could get to the hotel and get everything in shape for the exhibition, we had kept that big audience waiting for more than an hour. It was 9 o'clock at least when the curtain went up, and our boat left at 11 o'clock, and we were obliged to take this boat, as we were due in Brooklyn the next night. So we saw at once that we would have to rush the entertainment. Now, as everybody knows, the audience has to help make the show, for the "Great Unknown" is obliged to have victims from the audience to vent its power on. Unfor-

tunately the entertainment would not rush, for though
our manager begged, and pleaded, and argued with that
crowd of wealthy aristocracy, none of them would risk the
power of their muscle or their money against the power of
"The Great Unknown." In vain did he explain to them
that it was absolutely necessary for some of them to come
up to make the tests. At every other place the audience
was eager to accept such invitations. But tony Newport,
"Ah, don't cher know, Chawlie, I'm not a guy," wouldn't
come.

So there we were, plenty of power and nothing to run it
on. Time was precious, and we had spent thirty minutes
trying to get material from the audience, and all in vain.
Our management determined not to give up the big receipts
in the box-office, so my manager and my father had to offer
themselves as sacrificial victims to "The Great Unknown,"
to satisfy that obdurate crowd. I had always been called
the laughing girl, and I never could keep from laughing
when I saw big, strong men writhing under the influence
of the power, but, I must say, I never laughed as much in
my life as I did that night at my discomfited and tousled
father and manager. They were both always as nervous
about the "Power" as a bronco, about a threshing-machine,
and the didos they were made to cut up that night were too
ridiculous for expression. During these tests my father
would say to me in monotone, "Turn it on slow, Lulu, and
give it to me in broken doses." My manager also would beg
of me to "handle him carefully with right side up," and
when he took hold of the umbrella I heard him bid my
father "good-bye," as though the Power was going to trans-
port him to some unknown country. Had the little State of

Rhode Island (little as to area but big in everything else) been searched, no two persons could have been found upon whom the "Power" would act with greater force than upon my father and manager—why this was so I could never tell, but their strength was as naught when pitted against the power of "The Great Unknown."

I must say that the "Power" never had such a picnic as it did that night. But the performance hadn't gone on long before persons in the audience began to indicate dissatisfaction, and to imply that it was all put on, etc.; then my manager would retort back, "Well, sir, you just come up here and see if you can do any better than I am doing."

The consequence was in a short time we had a stage full of victims waiting for the slaughter; but then we had only thirty minutes in which to give them the tests. But the "Power" went through that crowd with a rush, like a whirlwind through a pile of dry leaves, and at the close we left them clamoring for more; but our boat was due to leave and we couldn't miss it. So we bade adieu to this wealthy and aristocratic resort to fill a week's engagement in the splendid Brooklyn theater at Brooklyn.

CHAPTER XVII.

BROOKLYN SUCCUMBS — "THE GREAT UN-KNOWN" AND THE WORLD RENOWNED JAPANESE WRESTLER, MATSADA.

He Falls before the Invincible — The Furore at Long Branch — On Sunday, August 12, 1884, an Earthquake and the Power Meet at Long Branch — Which was it That Shook the Big Hotel? — Differences of Opinion in the New York Papers.

Our wonderful triumph in New York fully insured the successful issue of our week's engagement in Brooklyn. It was everything we could have desired. The crowds were great, and fun, mystery and wonderment held the boards night after night. It would be superfluous for me to go into detailed accounts of these exhibitions.

The same tests were used as before described, with the same results. Nothing of very unusual interest occurred here, unless it was when the world-renowned Japanese wrestler, Matsada, came on the stage to pit his herculean strength and masterful skill against "The Great Unknown." Like Prof. Lafflin of New York, he was a magnificent specimen of physical manhood. He and Prof. Lafflin each are reputed to have a lift of 1,300 pounds with one hand. His interpreter accompanied him on the stage and made known the tests. The audience was all attention and suppressed excitement. He took the chair in his strong arms and pressed it to his breast with so much strength that I could hear the chair creak and see it writhe and show signs of dissolution. I placed my hands on the chair in the usual position and waited. "The Great Unknown" delayed its coming for some reason a little longer than usual. The audience grew more nervous and wrought up every moment.

It was a habit with me in making these tests to often pass one of my hands through my bangs (for these adornments were worn then), and many people thought this had something to do with my power. So, as I stood facing the stalwart Japanese, waiting for the on-coming of the Power, I passed my hands through my bangs, and this was no sooner done than that almond-eyed son of the east began to quiver and stagger, as though he had suddenly taken on a jag. I never will forget the strange, weird, superstitious look he gave me when he first felt the premonitory palsy that accompanies the approach of "The Great Unknown." Presently he began a grand dance around the stage, crushing the helpless chair as a partner in his mighty embrace, and as the power increased he *lost all control of himself, and seemed paralyzed with fear.* He was dashed from one side of the stage to the other, upsetting the chairs and overturning the scenery. He seemed to think that his only hope was to get my hands off the chair (" and thus break the current "). To accomplish this he turned suddenly toward his interpreter and shrieked out a bit of Eastern tongue, which his interpreter said was:

"Stop her! Stop her! Don't let her put her hands on the chair. She is worse than lightning." He retired completely vanquished.

During the enactment of this exciting scene every man, woman and child stood on their feet and yelled and shrieked at the top of their voices. They tossed up hats, handkerchiefs, canes and umbrellas in their wild enthusiasm. Pandemonium took possession of everybody and everything. It was a scene never to be forgotten, and I have never witnessed the like anywhere before or since.

Among a large number of accounts of our performances in Brooklyn, I will quote from a column write-up in the Brooklyn *Times* of the night of my contest with Matsada, headed :

"LULU AND MATSADA.

"The Georgia Wonder Meets the Great Japanese Wrestler, and Shakes ' Our John.' "

" There was the usual overflowing, shouting crowd in the Brooklyn Theater last night, and the cues and canes and chairs, with the fifteen or twenty assorted men who martyred themselves for the cause of science, went waltzing across the floor with the customary mad dance. The usual exciting scenes with wrecked umbrellas, canes and cues took place until the feature of the evening was introduced, the struggle over the chair by the Georgia Wonder and the celebrated Japanese wrestler, Matsada.

" The Oriental Orlando struggled and tugged, and did his level best, while Lulu, calm and smiling, dashed the Japanese around the stage amid the shouts and plaudits of an excited house. The audience went wild in their wrought-up enthusiasm over this wonderful and exciting scene.

"Then Matsada and four helpers clinging to the chair could not force it to the floor, and when the almond-eyed son of the East came back to his box he was heated, tired, panting and exhausted, while his fair antagonist was apparently as cool and fresh as ever.   *   *   *   *

"Then an invitation for the heavy weights to come upon the stage was extended by Mr. Atkinson, the manager, and the house rose to the enthusiasm of a full-fledged political mass-meeting, when the portly form of Ex-Assistant District Attorney John Oakey, 'our John,' was seen walking the plank. Mr. Oakey selected a stronger chair than the cane-bottomed one already dropsical through hard service. Miss Lulu placed her open palm against the chair post and the ex-assistant district attorney was lifted and bumped and rattled in a way that evidently brought conviction to the genial John, for in response to vociferous demands for a speech, he advanced to the front and said soberly: 'Well, all I can say is that's the first time I've ever been *shook* by a girl,' a remark which the house cheered to the echo. . . . . Miss Hurst's engagement concludes with to-morrow night's appearance, and whatever the outcome, she has afforded a novel and entertaining week, that at least those heroic souls who have sought to cope with her Power will not speedily forget."
*   *   *   *   *   *   *   *   *   *

From Brooklyn we went to Long Branch, and stopped at the Ocean House, owned and controlled by that prince of hotel managers, Mr. W. Leland. We had a pleasant visit here, and enjoyed the delightful hospitality of Mr. Leland. He took a great interest in the "Power," and was exceedingly kind to us all, and entertained us at his private cottage, where he insisted, after a long drive, on giving us a sample of his famous "apple-jack." His hospitality was so genuine and lavish that one could hardly refuse anything he suggested. But the "apple-jack" was rather a stunner for "Deacon Hurst," although I really think if my mother had not been present he would have enjoyed it, but knowing her great dislike for anything that even smacks of intoxicants, he would like to have refused it, but he could not. He often afterwards would tease my mother, by saying: "Well, I wish old Brother Leland would come along again with his famous apple-jack."

I was somewhat impressed with Long Branch during our stay there, and a comparison of it with Saratoga and Newport was naturally suggested to my mind. It was the fashion to speak of Long Branch as the American Brighton, but Brighton it certainly was not (judging from what I have read of this famous resort), and will never be, until the barn-like frame buildings, which serve it as hotels, are pulled down and others of more enduring and imposing appearance erected. It is these sprawling wooden structures which give to Long Branch that cheap and tawdry air and ginger-bread appearance, at which solid old Newport and substantial Saratoga sniff with scorn. But Long Branch is *sui generis;* and it is perhaps better in accord with the spirit of American institutions than any other of our watering-places. It is more republican than either Newport or Coney Island, because within its bounds the extremes of our life meet more freely. It is not so aristocratic as Newport, yet the President of the United States once lived there, and so do many other prominent examples of our political, literary, artistic, commercial, and social life. It is not so democratic as Coney Island, yet the poorer and more ignorant classes are largely represented throughout the season,

On hot Sundays there come to Long Branch great throngs of cheap excursionists, small tradesmen and artisans, with their families, with a sprinkling of roughs and sharpers—just such throngs as also go to Coney Island on the same day. Long Branch has equal attractions for rich and poor. It is quite astonishing with what ease the millionaire can get rid of dollars there, and it is almost equally astonishing what cheap and comfortable quarters are at the command of the humblest purses.

We gave our exhibitions in the big dining-room of the hotel, which would accommodate some 1,500 people. Two funny incidents happened while we were here. One night the house was packed, and the entertainment had been a grand success, but there were a few skeptics; and after the performance was over, a party of young men, who might be termed "Smart Alecks," remained, and in a boisterous way tried to prove to *their* satisfaction that the whole thing was a fraud, or rather, that it was muscular power. There were some six or seven of them in the party, and they seemed to be a species of "high-rollers," who had a great opinion of themselves.

We listened patiently to their jabber and badinage for awhile, until finally their manner became unbearable, and my manager lost his self-control, and rushing into the midst of them, he seized the spokesman by the collar and shook him until his cravat came off. It was a very rash and foolish thing for him to do. We had no friends present, and the audience had all left, and we were there alone, but it made no difference to him. They had intimated that we were palming off on the public one thing when we knew it to be another. He told the spokesman of the crowd as he shook him that he could not insult us, even if he did have a gang with him. There was no fight in them, but the result of the unpleasant affair was that they all came to time in quick order, and were as pleasant as they could be after this. We regretted this unpleasant occurrence, but realized that we had to protect ourselves from all unfair insinuations.   *   *   *   *   *

The other incident was of quite a different order from this, and was also of an exciting nature. On Sunday, August 12, 1884, at 3 P. M., a genuine, live, pulsating *earthquake* struck Long Branch broadside, and shook up the whole place as thoroughly as the "Power" had shaken up many of its inhabitants. As soon as the shock occurred, the resort was in a tumult of excitement, and all the visitors were making excited inquiries about the phenomenon, and it was but a short while before many of them in the house were claiming that Lulu Hurst had done it, and my room was soon besieged with visitors—so much so that I was forced to proceed to the parlors, where I could entertain the crowd and deny the allegation with as much sport and hilarity as I could. Of course, I knew there was no one present so silly as to really think that the "Power" had shaken the big hotel, but the fact that the house had been shaken, and that the "Power" was present at the time, and that this Power had so thoroughly shaken so many of the occupants beforehand, were suspicious facts and deemed worthy of consideration and comment.

A special to the New York *World*, dated August 15th, under the heading "Long Branch Notes," said:

"The summer capital has experienced many shocks this season, but the earthquake of Sunday outdid them all.

The cause of that earthquake has not yet been determined, at least Long Branchers claim that it has not. The ladies attribute it to the arrival of Miss Hurst, and that theory has much to back it, as the 'Power' was on the iron pier at the time, and it is asserted that her hands were on the rails, and if she could throw Warren Leland over, and he weighs 350 avoirdupois, they argue that she ought by the shaking of the pier to move the earth."

Another special to the New York *Tribune* says:

"Did I feel the earthquake? Well, rather. The walls shook and the windows rattled. Did Lulu Hurst do it? One of the guests at the Hotel said: 'To tell you the truth I didn't feel much of a shock. What I observed most was that my fellow inhabitants of this hostelry seemed to be in a great mess about something or other. I said to myself: What in the thunder is it all about? Has the Power of the Georgia Wonder broken loose? You know we had Miss Hurst here last night, and she made things decidedly lively. I thought at the moment that perhaps she had put her palm on the hotel balcony somewhere, and was making the whole concern jump. * * * * I saw her shortly after the reputed earthquake, or whatever it was, surrounded by an excited crowd, and I said to her: You didn't have anything to do with this row, did you, Miss Hurst? She smiled knowingly and observed: Ask Mr. Atkinson, he knows.'

"So we leave this matter by asking, what was it?"

CHAPTER XVIII.

"THE GREAT UNKNOWN."

The Rage in Buffalo—How the Georgia Wonder Unmasked the Fraudulent "Slate-Writing Medium"—Some Serious Reflections—The Pall of Universal Superstition Oppresses My Mind.

After leaving Long Branch we made our way toward Buffalo, and here we gave several entertainments at Central Music Hall. We were never in any city, New York not excepted, where the "Power" created greater excitement than in Buffalo. Our audiences were immense and remarkably enthusiastic, and every paper in the city devoted column after column to the discussion of the "Power" and its phenomena. Asking pardon of my readers, if I weary them, I will quote an editorial from the Buffalo *Times*, with the heading, "The Supernatural":

"The Georgia Wonder is beyond question a great curiosity. Her latent powers have baffled experts, scientists, professors and test committees, and she still remains a Wonder indeed.

"The exhibition at Music Hall last evening, like similar performances in other places, both amused and astonished the audience. That an ordinary country-raised girl, modest, retiring and apparently unsophisticated, should possess the marvelous power that was developed seems most remarkable. It is something more than ordinary physical strength. It is abnormal or supernatural.

"Skeptics and wiseacres may theorize and philosophize, but their theories are as unintelligent as the demonstration itself. Miss Hurst's powers are perhaps akin to other similar developments known as spiritualism, mesmerism, magnetism, clairvoyance and other abnormal manifestations. These things have astonished the people for years, and they remain a mystery yet.

"The fact is that man knows but little of the forces of nature or of the supernatural. It will not do to say that these singular developments are in harmony with nature's laws, as popularly understood, and that they are susceptible of scientific explanation. Spiritualists find a solution for mysterious raps, table-tipping, furniture-moving and slate-writing in alleging communion with disembodied spirits. Scientists pretend that a mesmeric influence is the cause of the apparently supernatural events; skeptics are content to call it a humbug. But none of these answers are satisfactory. Spiritualism gives us no proof except reputed communications from the other world that come through most remarkable 'mediums' and by strange devices. Science gives only a Bunsby opinion and looks wise, while the unbeliever scouts and denounces the whole thing as a trick and a fraud.

"The Georgia Wonder *has more power in her little finger* than the combined strength of three or four stalwart men. What is the world to do about it? Are we on the eve of an age of development that shall produce greater wonders than the world ever saw?

" ' Tis not safe to brush all these things aside with the charge of necromancy or sleight of hand. Until some satisfactory answer can be given to these manifestations, *the popular mind will crave a solution of them.* These things are not more a mystery than the possibilities of electricity were half a century ago. It is only forty years, the present year, since a United States senator proposed to incarcerate Prof. Morse for claiming that he could transmit intelligence from Washington to Baltimore, a distance of 40 miles, over a wire strung between the two cities. The process and philosophy of the thing are now well and generally understood. * * * *

"Would it be a greater wonder if some intelligence should elucidate the phenomena of messages coming from a source claimed to be beyond this life? As yet, it has not been done and it never may be. But is it wisdom and sufficient answer to these phenomena to cry humbug and fraud?

"The Georgia Wonder has been submitted to rigid tests, has passed through trying ordeals, and she remains a mystery. Those who claim that her power is only the exhibition of unusual physical strength betray their ignorance and confess their stupidity. They will fare little better in decrying this abnormal phenomenon than did the Indian who lassoed the locomotive on the plains, and fastened one end of the lariat to his body. A small piece of red man was found at the end of the cord when the train reached the next station."

I have quoted this editorial for several reasons. I want to show that the phenomena of the "Power" were classed everywhere with that of the most mysterious of the so-called occult or spiritualistic supernaturalism.

In fact, the New York *World* stated that the seances of the celebrated Home were tame in comparison with the wonders of the "Power." And the tone of the press over the entire continent was to the same effect. The "Power" was termed " odic, psychic, mesmeric, spiritistic," etc., and I was classed with celebrated "psychics" and abnormal "mediums," ancient and modern. My phenomena seemed to carry the minds of the people as by storm into these ab-normal ideas and supernatural domains. This leads me to say here, in anticipation of what the "Explanation" will disclose in full, that while I did not at the time understand and comprehend the course, nature and *raison d'être* of the Power, yet I did not believe it to be spiritistic, for the "ism" called " spiritism" (more commonly denoted " spir-itualism " and improperly so) was contrary to all my ideas of sense, reason and the natural order of things. Hence I always disliked the idea of the phenomena of the Power being so classed.

I will state in this connection that I think Buffalo has more "spiritualists" than any city we visited. They were strongly in evidence at our exhibitions, and as callers at our hotel. Usually, we found them very intelligent people, but in my opinion, how deluded!

It was here we saw a so-called "spirit medium," who gave " table-rapping " and " slate-writing " tests—(I wish I could now recall his name)—and we *caught up with him in his trickery.* He professed to give messages from disembodied spirits through these tests. I at once detected his manipulation in producing the "table-rapping" test, and promptly exposed it, but after I had exposed the "slate-writing test," which I will now describe.

He · hung a slate on my chest, which he *thoroughly cleaned to all appearances* (but which as we found afterwards had been "fixed" with a preparation which when *dry would show the writing already placed there*.) Well, in a few minutes I heard the *pencil writing!* My sense of hearing is as acute as a deer's, and I at once recognized the fact that the writing sound *did not come from the double slates which were on my chest*. I began to cast my eyes around to locate the sound, and I saw the "Medium" jerk his foot! I kept still and in a moment the writing sound began again. I then cast my eyes down suddenly, and lo! the wonderful "Medium" was scratching a small piece of slate on the floor with a tack or some such object under his shoe.

It was a dead, clear case of "give-away," and he returned my $3.00 I had paid him for the "séance," and I left him a discomfited and sadder, if not a wiser, man. This then, thought I, is *e pluribus unum* of this class of so-called "Wonderful Phenomena," by which so many innocent people are constantly deluded. This incident made a great impression on my mind, and caused me to seriously reflect on how the phenomena of my "Power" were helping to prepare people's minds to be more easily and effectually duped by all such fraudulent tricksters, who incessantly apply such arts of delusion, under the false garb of communion with the sacred dead. It made me resolve anew that if ever I fathomed and understood the phenomena of my "Power," so that I could explain and demonstrate it, I would do so when that opportune time came, and help to clear up the minds of the people on all these notions of so-called "oc-cultism" with which my manifestations were classed. I was satisfied that all such that were not artful trickery, would, at some time, be reduced to their proper sensible and natural categories.

I was much impressed with the many conditions which were imposed upon us while we were thus searching for spiritualistic phenomena, such as joining of hands, darkening of rooms, cabinets, etc. But young and inexperienced as I was, I had unshaken confidence in the positiveness of all natural laws. I viewed everything by nature's rules, which are never set aside by freak nor accident, and whose laws are never abrogated. I knew that natural science and spiritualistic observation stand directly opposed to each other—on the one side stands the authority of the whole history of science, the totality of all known natural laws, which have been discovered under the presumption of a universal causality; and the other announces the discovery that causality has a flaw, and by this flaw we are told that the laws of gravitation, of electricity, of light, and of heat, are altogether of a hypothetical validity; they have authority as long as the inexplicable spiritualistic something does not cross them.

The science of philosophy cannot be without danger of having its reputation damaged, when you throw overboard all principles of scientific investigation, in order to find in the revelations of "rapping spirits" the means of supplementing our insight into the order of the world. What is to become of philosophy? Whence is the scientific investigator to get courage and perseverance for his work, if the laws of nature can be dispensed with? And who will be

10 l

inclined to occupy himself with scientific problems when he is allured by the hope of obtaining an answer to the deepest and highest questions by means of spiritualistic appearances? The time may come when you will pay a so-called "medium" three dollars, and thus induce him to call forth your dear departed, who will execute mechanical performances, such as rapping on tables, playing on musical instruments, writing you sweet messages, etc. But remember when you hear the raps, read the message, or hear the music, that it will be brought about by no flaw in nature, but through some flaw or superstition in you.

Such thoughts as these engaged my mind after leaving this crestfallen "medium"; and when I see the world filled with blind superstition it oppresses me the more, and I long for the time to come when I may be able to correct at least such of these superstitions as I myself have occasioned.

I will close the account of our stay in Buffalo with a few quotations from the voluminous and numerous articles that were written about our performances there.

From a column account in the Buffalo *Times*:

"That Miss Lulu Hurst's performance was appreciated on the first appearance is amply testified by the largely increased audience at Music Hall last night, as well as the character of the same. Among those present interested in the Wonderful Girl's accomplishments were scientists, physicians and professional men, who came to fathom the unparalleled and phenomenal feats. An element of sympathy seemed to prevail among the fair sex, for a greater part of the audience were ladies, who must have carried from the hall the impression that Miss Hurst was an ornament to the sex. * * * * * * *

"Among the number who tested the Power on the stage were Mr. Young, Clerk of Vital Statistics, Mr. Fornes, wholesale merchant, John C. Scott, Attorney Feldman, and Dr. Bownan of Boston, who seemed to have come armed with the opinion that the agency employed was merely physical force, and resolved to show to the audience that his opinion was the correct theory; he signally failed, however, and it was clearly demonstrated to the audience's satisfaction, if not to his, that the Power is something outside the domains of the physical, whether it is electrical, spiritualistic or will force, we cannot say.

"When the curtain rose on the second act another scramble was made for the chairs, and amid the confusion Dr. Bownan arose to advance his theory of how Miss Hurst resisted the combined efforts of half a dozen men to force a billiard cue to the floor while the Wonder placed the palm of her right hand under it. He sagely contended that it was done by placing it under her arm, and when the experiment was again tried it was seen that her arm did not close upon it at all, and further, to prove that there was no mechanical contrivance, a strong walking cane from the audience was used. Dr. Van Peyma was among the second detachment on the stage, and to the many phenomena of this act he gave the strictest scrutiny of the position of the lady's hands and to the relaxation and contraction of the hands of the performers, and yet he was completely baffled. During the operation of attempting to hold the chair-still, there was a request by some one, to turn to the audience, and this was done, and soon after the chair and its possessors were cutting ludicrous antics across the stage, and the scene finally wound up by the gentlemen having a narrow escape from being thrown headlong over the footlights. This was followed by five of the heaviest weights attempting to force the chair to the floor with the usual result," etc.

The Buffalo *Courier* in a thrilling account says: "The large number of gentlemen who undertook to put their physical strength against the strange Power of the Wonder, found themselves as powerless as a canary bird in a cyclone," etc.

The same paper in another long article says: "Those who witnessed her remarkable performances were more than ever impressed with the idea that wonders will never cease. Many had come determined to fathom the mysterious power by the aid of which Miss Hurst performed her wonderful feats, but we have yet to hear of one who was not nonplussed in his efforts. Time after time did this fair young girl with the utmost nonchalance resist the combined strength of the most powerful men."

The Buffalo *Times* in one of its articles says:

"To say that she accomplishes *wonders* is not going beyond the bounds of truth; this was clearly demonstrated by the fact of having the combined strength of four powerful men opposed to what appeared to be a simple touch of her hands. She prevented the strongest person from keeping any object at rest by simply placing the palms of her hands against the object.   *   *   *   *   *

"What adds to the mystery and interest of the whole proceedings is the ease and delight with which this truly wonderful girl accomplishes all her feats."

The Buffalo *Express* also gave a number of full accounts of the doings of the Power, which it classed as "marvelous and incomprehensible."   *   *   *   *   *

The following beautiful poem, in tribute to myself, was written by the well known and versatile poet, Mr. E. P. Whipple, of the Buffalo *Times*, and presented to me by him in Central Music Hall. This evidence of his good will and esteem I appreciated more than I can express:

LINES TO LULU·HURST.

Wondrous Girl! what mystic power is thine!
　So strange—so marvelous too,
'Twould seem as if the lightning's power
　Were given of God to you
For some great purpose—unrevealed,
　But which in days near by
Shall be disclosed to you in light
　By Him who reigns on high.

What power is thine, pure, gentle girl?
　Do hosts of angels stand
Unseen around thy presence here,
　A mighty, heavenly band?
No mortal eye doth view that sight
　Of host and army strong
That walk with thee and talk with thee,
　A bright angelic throng.

I seem to see them bending low,
　With outstretched wing and arm,
Your life to shield from ills below
　And keep you safe from harm.
How loving is their presence here,
　Their help, how sweet, divine—
How blessed that one on whom·their smiles
　Of love and beauty shine.

Not yet, dear child, are you to know
　All reason for your power,
Which now in mere material things
　Makes wonder for the hour.

But as this subtle force reveals
  Its strength from day to day,
I think you'll find that God's own hand
  In you shall find display.

Some mission sweet, some work for good,
  He's chosen you to do.
He's called you here—a hand-maid help—
  Coworker with Him too.
Something he wants in future years
  Performed by hand of love,
And so on you descends a power
  From Him, our God above.

Already on kind mission bent,
  Your dear, blessed hand of love
Hath done some work appointed you
  By Him, thy God above:
For loving was that kindly act
  Of which I read one day,
The little church with struggling debt
  Your gift did sweetly pay.

Dear blessed girl! thou favored child,
  So honored high of God,
So blessed of angels round the throne,
  Thou chosen of the Lord!
Oh, consecrate thy power to Him,
  And thank Him every hour,
That royal robes of heavenly strength
  Clothe you with angel's power.

When I behold that wondrous power,
  So strange, displayed by thee,
Methinks on earth, in human guise
  An angel I do see.
They came to Abraham in his day,
  To Isaac and to Noah,
And why not now to us on earth,
  To us who need them sore.

Sweet, gentle girl, thy wondrous gift,
  To thee so grandly given,
Comes not of earth; a blessing 'tis
  Conferred on thee from Heaven.
A talent 'tis of rare endow,
  Annointing thee with power.
Use well that talent, precious child,
  In this thy day and hour.

From Buffalo we went on a visit to Niagara Falls, and from there home for a short rest, before taking a journey to the far west and the Pacific slope.

CHAPTER XIX.

THE "POWER" ON THE BORDERS OF THE PA-
CIFIC—THE SHOCK SHAKES SAN FRAN-
CISCO.

*Mr. H. de Young's Wild Rush through a Chandelier—The
Gallant Members of the City Press Meet their Waterloo.*

" The Great Unknown " " bobbed up serenely " in San
Francisco in the beautiful month of September (the most
delightful part of the year here) and held undisputed sway
for a week. Mr. Chas. Frohman had arranged for our appearance at the Metropolitan Hall, the largest and handsomest
building of its kind in the city. We had pleasant apartments
at the Baldwin Hotel, and the many kind attentions shown
us there added much to the pleasure of our happy sojourn
in this lovely city. It was in the handsome dining-room
of this splendid hotel that we gave our first exhibition on
the Pacific coast. This was a "Press Exhibition," but
many of the leading citizens were present, and among them
were: Mrs. W. H. de Young, Mrs. Joe Austin, Miss
Mamie Deane, Miss Mollie Stege, Mrs. W. M. Bunker,
Mrs. Frank Unger, Mrs. Al Hayman, Mrs. Turnbull, Mrs.
J. R. Jackson, Mrs. W. H. Walker, Major-General Turnbull, Mr. W. H. de Young, Dr. Brigham, Mr. A. B. Hen-

derson, Mr. J. Ross Jackson, Mr. J. Crighton, Mr. James Williamson, Mr. Frank Ballinger, Mr. T. J. Vivian, Mr. Porter Robertson, Mr. H. M. Burke, Mr. M. Gunst, Mr. Alexander Von Huhn, Mr. T. T. Williams, Mr. W. M. Bunker, Mr. W. H. Bunker, Mr. Al Hayman, Mr. Fred Engelhart, Mr. Harry Brown, Dr. Chisholm, Dr. McAllister, J. M. Ward, Mr. H. H. Pearson, Mr. J. P. Bogardus, Mr. Otto Tum Suden, Mr. H. Herrmann, and many other leading citizens. The dining-room had been cleared for the occasion, but, to quote a clause from the *Examiner's* account, " This spacious room was rather a careless selection, as events proved, for mirrors and chandeliers had several narrow escapes."

We found that the people on the distant Pacific coast were just as eager to see the " Wonderful Power," and seemed as well posted concerning its marvelous manifestations, as if we had been in the presence of a Georgia or New York audience—all going to show that the press of the coast had been keeping their readers fully posted about the "Wonder Worker" of the distant East.

They were fully prepared for anything, and their interest was as keen as could be.

Mr. Al Hayman, the great theatrical manager of the West, had charge of our exhibition in this city. One of our friends, and our most efficient champion here, was Mr. H. de Young, proprietor and editor of the San Francisco *Chronicle.* No one stood higher in the estimation of the people than he did. He was to California what the great and lamented Grady was to Georgia—gifted both as a writer and an orator, and unexcelled as an entertainer.

Mr. de Young took a lively interest in the " Power,"

and it did him up in fine shape. Fully 2,000 people saw our first exhibition there, and during our week's entertainment we had as large audiences as we could have possibly desired.

The newspapers of the city were lavish in their accounts of the doings of the "Power." There was not one that did not devote column after column to the subject. The following is from one of the *Chronicle's* articles :

"Probably the most puzzled concourse of people that ever left a public building in this city were the thousand or more ladies and gentlemen who issued from Metropolitan Hall last night, where they had seen half a hundred of their own numbers test the 'Power' of Lulu Hurst, the Georgia Wonder. All were discussing and disputing, but none felt themselves able to explain whether what they had seen savored of the supernatural, or the natural, or whether she was some strangely endowed being sent to refute Bob Ingersoll's doctrine that there is nothing in heaven or on earth which cannot be made plain with the aid of logic."

The folowing is the *Alta* account of the umbrella test with Mr. H. de Young, proprietor of the *Chronicle:*

"Mr. H. de Young, proprietor of the *Chronicle*, was one of the volunteers, and engaged in the umbrella test. This was a remarkable feature of the evening's entertainment, and was what might be termed 'flirting under an umbrella.' But before he got through all romantic sentiment, together with the ribs of the umbrella, were a total wreck. The umbrella was opened and Mr. de Young and the Georgia Wonder gathered themselves under its commodious shelter, each grasping the handle. In an instant the folds flapped over their heads and coiled around their necks, as if endowed with steel springs, and in another moment the movement was reversed, and the umbrella was turned inside out and went sailing through the air on invisible wings, both parties still clinging to it and apparently unable to release their grasp.

"When the aerial voyagers were finally rescued, the rain-shedder had outlived its usefulness, and resembled a Blaine boomlet caught in a Cleveland simoon."

The *Alta* also says:

"There is something unexplainable about the phenomenal exhibition of power by Miss Lulu Hurst. . . . . She is one skeptics should see and scientists should try to unravel the mystery."

From the *Chronicle* article we quote the account below of some tests with the newspaper men:

"Peter Robertson, of the *Chronicle*, was the first man who attempted to resist the gigantic power of Lulu Hurst. When the 'Force' struck him he flew around the room as though a cyclone had been turned loose. What he had undertaken to do seemed simple and easy enough. He grasped a light cane-seated chair tightly and clasped it to his breast with all his power. Miss Hurst was to force it to the floor. She laid her hand on the seat, and the other she held before her to hide her laughing face. There was a pause of a few seconds, and then Mr. Robertson and the chair began to wobble. The Wonder laughed, and then tried to look unconcerned. Mr. Robertson began to stagger around and then to whirl. The perspiration gathered on his brow in beads. As fast as he whirled Miss Hurst chased him around. . . . The dance grew more exciting. Mr.

Robertson flew about more wildly, and the Wonder's laugh could be heard all over the room.   Suddenly man and chair flew off into one corner, the Georgian still pursuing, and with a crash they landed against the wall.   Mr. Robertson pulled himself out, smiled nervously, and said, 'I am satisfied.'   *   *   *   *   *   *

"Then General Turnbull, of the *Alta*, stepped forward with a pale but determined face.   When the force began to operate on him he held his ground steadily, but his legs began to shake.   He staggered and tottered, but slowly and surely the chair sought the floor.   His utmost strength could not withstand the force of the calm, laughing girl who merely laid her hand on the chair.

"'I've had enough,' he said as he took his seat.

"Mr. T. T. Williams, another newspaper man, stepped forward next, and soon he was whirling around like a dervish.   'I might as well have tried to stop the flywheel of an engine,' he said.   'Her hand was like a five-ton weight on that chair.'

"John Chretien, Mr. Martinez and another gentleman exerted their combined strength to hold the chair up. They failed ignominiously.   When it reached the floor, 'Lift it up,' Mr. Atkinson, the manager, said.   The three men arched their backs over the chair and pulled.   It remained unmoved.   *   *   *   *   *   *

"The next feat was lifting a chair with Mr. H. de Young seated in it.   He deposited his 160 avoirdupois and awaited developments.   Miss Hurst placed the palms of her hands against the sides of the back of the chair, and without any apparent exertion lifted Mr. de Young and the chair three or four times clear off the floor.   She lifted Alex Von

Huhn, of the *Democrat*, so violently that he fell over on the floor. * * * * * *. *

"Several men, some weighing 200 pounds, were lifted with as little apparent effort."

In a two-column article the *Call* stated:

"The audience that assembled in Metropolitan Hall last night to witness the performances of Miss Lulu Hurst, the girl of mysterious power, revealed in its numbers, as well as its average character for intelligence, an interest in the matter that is not entertained in the minds of the community with regard to the mummeries and hackneyed manifestations of the so—called science of spiritualism.* More than one-third of the audience was composed of ladies. Many of our best citizens, judges, members of the learned professions and scientists were there with their families. . .

"Some of the experimenters briefly told of their experiences and impressions. They said they could neither explain nor resist the power Miss Hurst exerted. One man, with a thin face, long hair brushed up from his forehead, commenced by saying that when he took the cue, and after Miss Hurst laid her hand upon it, he felt something like electricity, though the feeling was finer than that produced by electricity, passing up his arms, and he was pushed back by a force that did not appear to be exerted by the lady. 'He would call it a psychic force, and it was exerted by spirits, not by one spirit alone, but by a band of spirits acting in concert.' Here the audience saw at once that the man was a dyed-in-the-wood spiritualist and they hissed and hooted him down. * * * * *

" 'It seemed to me like holding back a wild bronco,' said a stout young man after experimenting with the Wonder and a chair.

"Denis Kearney, who tried to hold the chair, attributed its motion to muscular force.

"John P. McMurry stated that he detected no muscular demonstration on Miss Hurst's part.

"The greater number saw in the power some occult influence, something unexplained and unexplainable."

In conclusion, I will quote the following from a long article in *The Ingleside* published in this city :

"LULU HURST.

"The Georgia Wonder"—The Human Puzzle of the Nine-teenth Century.

"As a matter of fact, Miss Hurst's powers have a right to the term wonderful.   The world is full of wonders, which, being accepted, named and classified, no longer excite public curiosity.   Miss Hurst astonishes us more than the development of a plant, the earthquake, the birth of a butterfly, or the transmission of a telegraphic message, not because she is more mysterious, but because she is an isolated case.

CHAPTER XX.

AN EPIDEMIC OF "HURSTOMANIA."

The Assault on Mormondom—Other Miracles than the Great Unknown.

From San Francisco we went to Sacramento where the State Fair was in progress. Here we had the usual crowds, and the same success we met with everywhere. We also exhibited in a number of other cities, and then spent a week in Oakland. At this place the whole town went "daft" on "Hurstomania," as the papers there termed the craze after the Power.

One of the papers says, in a long and splendidly written article, headed

"HURSTOMANIA.

"*A Town full of Liluchondriacs Monkeying with Broomsticks, Umbrellas and Kitchen Chairs:*

"Oakland has gone daft. The 'Odic Force' is upon us. Old 'Psychic Power' is among us and she bids fair to become as obnoxious as the esthetic craze, the blue-glass absurdity or the fifteen puzzle idiocy. At one time it look-ed as though we were about to be afflicted with the Inger-

(159)

soll refutation mania, but the 'Wonder' came to us in time to divert the stream of metaphysical disputation that threatened to overwhelm the social fabric. We welcome the 'Georgia Wonder' with her contagious mirth-provoking giggle as a joyous relief from the impending danger, but like the congregation who prayed for rain, we did not bargain for a deluge.

Everybody has quit doing anything else, and is now engaged in the pleasurable occupation of refuting Lulu Hurst. Every advocate of every theory regarding the sources of her power is boring his friends with an exposition of the same. The languid dude and the stable boy, the capitalist and the peanut-vendor, the merchant and the mendicant, the professional man and the artisan, are all experimenting with umbrellas, billiard cues, chairs, etc. In the boudoir and kitchen, in the office and club, men and women, are devoting their energies dragging each other hither and thither by means of sticks, chairs and gingham umbrellas. *   *   *   *   *   *

"The theory that the chair test is a 'conservation of forces,' whatever that may mean, is being learnedly demonstrated by the scientific athletes of the Athenian Club, and the evenings at that symposium are devoted to practical explanations of 'how the thing is done.' The available chairs have all been rendered comparatively useless, save for experimental purposes. The weakest man in the club, who shall be 'nameless here forevermore,' has submitted himself incessantly to the ordeal of holding a chair in a certain position while the majority of the directory pile themselves upon it, determined to drag it down or perish in the attempt. Other muscular Athenians are at the same time waltzing around the assembly hall attached to other chairs propelled by other weak Athenians, while several lecturers are expounding extempore addresses, explanatory of the leverage necessary to produce an equilibrium of force. The Athenian Club is at present an Isthmian arena, and the gods smile gratefully. * * * * *

"And the end is not yet. The climax has not been reached.

"Even the Muses have been evoked to add variety to the scene and rhymesters abound."

And another paper writes:

"Everybody has an explanation of the phenomena and nobody is satisfied with that explanation.

" 'Odic Force,' learnedly explains the elderly gentleman whose vision was impaired by sitting up o' nights reading the odes of the German philosopher. The elderly gentleman then proceeds to explain what odic force is, and when he concludes his hearers feel as if they had taken a plunge bath in the Pierian Spring.

" 'Psychic Force' remarks the disciple of the Concord School of Philosophy, and then he delivers his little speech explanatory of this force, which is somewhat clearer than mud and exceedingly convincing." * * * *

We bade adieu to California with its gold and its golden fruit, and went up through Idaho, Montana, Nevada, visiting and exhibiting in many of the larger towns, such as Helena, Butte City, Anaconda, Deer Lodge, etc., thence down to Salt Lake City where we gave three exhibitions to crowded houses.

The power was just as potent in knocking out "Mormon elders" as it had been in handling Georgia crackers or

New York athletes.   Mormon women were just as full of curiosity about the power as other woman.   And I really think
if their Prophet and King, Brigham Young, had returned
to the quaint old town, his presence would not have created
more talk and excitement than did the advent of the "Great
Unknown."

From the governor of the little State, who was entertained at a private exhibition, on down to the humblest
citizen, they were all alike amazed and mystified.

One of the papers, *The News,* said:

"We have witnessed the exhibition of the powers of this
marvelous human phenomenon, and were thoroughly convinced, as were all present, that it is one of the most remarkable and inexplicable things that has yet dawned on
the horizon of science."

The *Salt Lake Chronicle,* in one of its lengthy articles,
says:

"Miss Lulu Hurst has been most appropriately called
'The Miracle of the Nineteenth Century.' . . . That she
is a phenomenon bordering on the supernatural is conceded
by all who see her exhibitions."

The Salt Lake *Herald* had this to say in one of its two-
columned articles:

"Those who have subjected themselves to the process say
that there is no sensation accompanying the force that
proceeds from the touch, so the term electricity is evidently
a misnomer.

"At the idea of spiritualism she herself laughs; it can
hardly be called magnetism.   The feeling that comes over
one when he finds himself being dashed and badgered about
is that if he only had more muscular strength, he would be

able to withstand it, but the most professional of athletes have been as sucklings in her hands. Salt Lake finds itself, as the sum total of all its cogitation, utterly without a reason that will account for what it has seen."

Another paper gave this view:

"This is my conclusion concerning the extraordinary powers of Miss Hurst.

"First. That she is no stronger than ordinary ladies of her size.

"Second. She has by the aid of electricity reached some means of partially stunning those with whom she comes in contact, when she wishes to do so.

"Third. Being thus weakened, she can overcome them while in that condition, and hence their weakness is imputed to her as strength; whereas she is not stronger but they are weaker. Other ladies can probably do the same, but no man. In exactly what way she operates the electricity I at present cannot tell; but I am certain she has it about her person."

*   *   *   *   *   *   *   *   *

Thus I might give hundreds and hundreds of opinions and explanations of the "Power" from the press all over the continent, advancing every sort of conceivable and inconceivable theory concerning it, but I fear of wearying the reader.

Many declared that the power was the "Miracle of the Nineteenth Century," but when I stepped into the office of the Rio Grande railroad at Salt Lake City, and spoke for the first time into a telephone, and was answered by the Agent at Ogden some sixty miles away, I was fully impressed that there were other "Miracles" than the "Great Unknown."

CHAPTER XXI.

DENVER, COLORADO, SHAKEN UP.

The Press Puzzled and Powerless—Governor Grant Thrown Off of His Dignity.

I will give the account of my four wonderful performances in Denver—for they were wonderful in more ways than one—by quoting accounts thereof from the enterprising newspapers of that city, which were extravagantly liberal in the space given in description of my exhibitions. I like to give these quotations from the press, not because of any egotism on my part, but to show the reader what critical, disinterested journals say, and so leave absolutely no room to doubt the absolute genuineness and truthfulness of everything recorded in this book. Of course I have to cull and abbreviate these accounts as much as possible, for if I were to publish all that were written about the "Power" over the continent it would fill more than a dozen large volumes.

Our first performance was a complimentary press exhibition, given to the newspaper men primarily, but any one desiring to do so could attend. We invariably gave these exhibitions in every city so that the lynx-eyed reporters and representatives and professional men could have every opportunity to see and test the power in all the details, of its manifestation.

The Denver *Tribune Republican* says:

"LULU HURST, THE ENIGMA.—*The Wonderful Girl Gives a Private Exhibition of Her Powers—She Laughs at the Combined Physical Powers of Muscular Men—Skeptics put to Sea.*

"About thirty ladies and gentlemen, among them journalists and prominent officials and citizens, assembled in the parlors of Charpiot's Hotel yesterday afternoon at 3 o'clock, to witness a private exhibition of the remarkable powers of the 'Georgia Wonder,' Miss Lulu Hurst. She gave this exhibition chiefly for the benefit of the members of the press, that they might be better satisfied as to the genuineness and honesty of the performance which she gives. That this performance is remarkable, extraordinary, inexplicable, marvelous, all those who were present yesterday afternoon will testify. That there is no trick about it, but that the power is as honest as it is remarkable was equally well demonstrated. Among those present who will verify these statements were Gov. Grant, Hon. Jas. Belford, Alderman E. J. Brooks, Phil Trounstine, Hon. Jno. C. Montgomery, Mr. D. W. Mann, Col. John Arkins, manager of the *News*, Mr. K. G. Cooper, Mr. O. H. Rothacker of *Opinion*, Managing Editor Hayward of the *Hyphen*, and many others."

Then follows a two-column account of the experiments, the article concluding: "This exhibition lasted about three quarters of an hour, and was one of the most entertaining and inexplicable performances that any one present ever witnessed. Probably the majority were skeptical when they went in, but there were no skeptics among those who emerged from the hotel an hour later. A stronger testimonial to the straightness of the exhibition cannot be uttered. * * * * While she is performing what appears to be her greatest physical feats, a smile is constantly playing upon her lips, and when her opponents begin dancing about the room under the influence of her inexplicable power, she laughs as heartily and appears to enjoy the ludicrousness of the situation as much as do any of her auditors. Then, too, at the conclusion of her test, while her contestants retire completely fagged out and gasping for breath, there is not noticeable about her any increased respiration or other sign of mental or physical exertion. She is well termed 'The Wonder of the Nineteenth Century.' "

I cannot resist quoting the following editorial by this same enterprising journal to show the contrariety of theories advanced to account for the "Force":

"Probably a great many wise heads and not a few foolish ones will give some thought to the subjects of animal magnetism and psychology, now that Lulu Hurst, the Georgia Phenomenon, is in Denver. We doubt that if one of them will arrive at an entirely satisfactory explanation of the wonderful things which she does. * * *

"There is something irresistibly funny as well as marvelous in the spectacle of a 250-pound man being swung around a big room by no other apparent force than the touch of a young girl's hands; to see an umbrella turned inside out as if struck by a cyclone, and the unfortunate victim who has hold of the handle precipitated into a corner.

"It is ridiculous to say that this young girl does these feats by main strength, for it would be simply impossible for any one person to be strong enough to resist the force of the number of muscular men who are at one time exerting all their strength to overcome the peculiar power or influence which she exercises.

"Is it animal magnetism? Is it psychology? Perhaps it is a little of both. Twenty years ago it might have been called spiritualism, indeed, it might be so-called to-day, and it very likely is by spiritualists. The power or combination of powers which this young girl possesses is not recognized by science except so far as it has to recognize it, although latter day philosophers have given much study to both psychology and animal magnetism. Now, it is easier to explain Miss Hurst's powers by saying that it is entirely psychology, meaning the force of mind over matter, than it is to account for it by calling it simply animal magnetism. If it were only animal magnetism it could not always be made operative against the strength of a strong man, though it could be made so over a piece of wood or other lifeless matter. But it is possible for a combination of the animal magnetism and the psychic force to accomplish the results which are shown us by Miss Hurst, provided these two forces are possessed in a remarkable degree. To simplify the proposition, it is not altogether beyond reason that this young girl can by the exercise of a strong will and the power of animal magnetism, which she undoubtedly has to a great degree, make passive matter do her bidding. Writers of psychology have cited instances of persons having this psychic or will force to such a phenomenal degree as to be able to will a table to move toward them without touching it.

"In the matter of psychology where live matter is acted upon, the temperament becomes a factor. To make a good subject for the psychologists, one must be of a lymphatic temperament. The slower the intellect works the better. We believe it to be true that Miss Hurst finds it more difficult to overcome a nervous strength than one which comes from physical or muscular power alone, even if they are both equal, considered as physical strength.

"It may be that the young man who acts as master of ceremonies of the exhibition has this psychic power and that he aids her in the work. This is not impossible, though it may be very wide of the mark. Then for that matter, the great power of this young lady may lie in some subtle trick. And all serious attempts to analyze it may yet prove to be farcical. But the fact remains that there is no complete explanation of this power."

The *Daily News* gave a long account of this press exhibition and concluded as follows :

"We have no explanation to offer. The girl did everything described without the slightest apparent effort, and there is not an athlete in the world who could duplicate her performance."

The Denver *Times* closes a long article by saying :

"She took hold of nothing. She merely laid her hands on it, and neither she nor the one who had hold of the object seemed to be able to control the motion of the object that followed. Among those present were Gov. Grant and a large majority of the editors of the city papers."

"Hon. Jas. B. Belford, member of Congress," says the Denver *Republican*, "after being hurled violently about clinging to a chair he was vainly trying to hold, stated to the audience:

" 'Ladies and gentlemen, I give it up. I was skeptical when I came up here, but now I give it up. This is something more than I can resist.' "

CHAPTER XXII.

HURSTOMANIA EPIDEMIC IN DENVER.

The Defeat of the Duplicators—A Challenge that was Never Accepted—The Vanquishment of the " City Hall Crowd " Led by "the Little Man"—A $500 to $250 Bet that Found no Takers.

One of the largest crowds we ever had was at Denver. On the second night of our performance there, before the box office of the theater was open, there was a line of people extending from the office out to the sidewalk and along the sidewalk for a block waiting for the office to open to get their tickets.

In Denver certain parties known as the " city hall crowd," headed by Alderman Maginn, took up the notion that the said alderman (whom the press dubbed " the little man") could duplicate my feats. They made their boasts and gave it wide circulation all over the city. Mr. Atkinson heard of it and at once issued a challenge to said "city hall crowd" and to " the little man " to make good their boasts, and offering to deposit in the box office $500 against $250 that they could not do so, the amount to be donated to any charitable institution in the city. This challenge was published in all the papers, and fully commented on by them all. The "city hall crowd" was told by the press to put up or shut up. "The little man" gave it out that their money was ready, and that they would be on hand the next night with plenty of power and a winning hand.

The following is a partial account by the *Tribune* of this very exciting evening's entertainment, headed :

"MISS HURST AND HER RIVALS."

"' The Little Man' and his City Hall Backers in a Predicament—They Attempt to Duplicate Miss Hurst's Performance and are Laughed at—Fun at the Academy.

"'Lulu Hurst is a fraud.' Such sentiment was expressed at the city hall yesterday without reserve. Alderman Maginn, the little man, about whose powers to duplicate Miss Hurst's acts so much has been said by the city hall people, was in and about City Clerk Speer's office all day, and gave such tests to his friends as to make them enthusiastic in singing his praises. The little alderman bore the marks of approbation meekly, and time and again offered to wager money that he could duplicate any one of Miss Hurst's performances.

"'Why, it's all trickery, muscular power,' City Clerk Speer repeated to each inquiring newcomer, and 'little man Maginn' will prove it to the satisfaction of everybody to-night. Mr. Speer was greatly excited over the developments, and flitted in and out of the various city offices in a bewildered sort of a way. Building Inspector Willoughby looked on stolidly. Judge Mullahey sat on his bench uneasily. Uncle Billy Beatty left it to his deputy

to look after the auditor's office, but Mr. Keefe had so
many official visits to pay to the city clerk's office that he
did not miss much that was going on. Clerk Raymond
stood around looking ponderous and mystified. Mayor
Routt peeped in at what was going on, shook his head
dubiously, and went up the street. Aldermen Kelby and
Bandhaur were firm believers in the suddenly developed
powers of their fellow-alderman, and clapped him on the
shoulder familiarly.

"In fact, the business of the city conducted itself yesterday.

"AT THE ACADEMY.

"At 8 o'clock last evening ' little man Maginn,' arm in
arm with City Clerk Speer, and followed by a dozen or
more city hall officials, was among the crowds of people
who were flocking to the Academy to see Miss Hurst and
her rivals in the mystic power. The doings of the city hall
people had spread to such an extent that the Academy
could not hold the crowd who went to see the trickery exposed. Alderman Maginn had under his arm a package
of cheap umbrellas, which he had purchased during the
afternoon, and with which he was going to duplicate the
umbrella act.

"Mr. Speer and his followers each carried something
which was to form a part of the exposé. The Academy
was packed, standing room and all.   *   *   *   *

"A few minutes past 8 o'clock Mr. Atkinson, the manager, stepped to the footlights and said he thanked the
people of Denver for the liberal patronage and past expressions of approbation. In no city had they met with a
warmer reception than in Denver. Wherever they went

they found a few skeptics and people who asserted that they could duplicate Miss Hurst's performances. Denver was no exception to the rule. Mr. Atkinson then referred to the city hall people, and said that he had had $500 deposited in the box office of the theater all the afternoon, but the little man and his friends had failed to come to time. They had utterly failed upon due notice to back up their vain boasting with their money. Why didn't they make $500 so easily, at the same time they were showing up Miss Hurst's performances? They had wanted her to do certain tricks, certain ways. He had written his challenge, of which the general public was informed, but the would-be rivals of Miss Hurst would not accede to these terms. She did not pretend to do certain feats. She did what she advertised, and Mr. Atkinson said that he was willing to bet at large odds that her performances could not be duplicated. He would say that at the close of Miss Hurst's performance an opportunity would be given for her would-be rivals to show what they could do." Then follows a full description of my performance, closing as follows :

" The chair test was no more successful for Miss Hurst's opponents than it was at other performances. C. Zeal, Billy Brewer, J. K. Ashby, Henry Cole, C. B. Brooks, and others, tried to hold the chair somewhere in the vicinity of the stage. The biggest tussle was given the Wonder by C. D. Brooks and Alderman Bandhauer. They broke two chairs before they got through, and Alderman Bandhauer's hands were bruised and bleeding, but they did not get the chair near the floor. Seven men tried to push it to the floor, but they did not succeed until Miss Hurst released her hold. Then it went to the floor with a crash."

Then follows statements by these experimenters to the audience giving their views of the Wonderful Power, as they termed it.   *   *   *   *   *   *   *

The article then goes on :

"THE LITTLE MAN TALKS.

"Alderman Maginn then took the stage. He said he had offered to bet money that he could duplicate Miss Hurst's feats, but her manager had failed to make a wager with him or his friends. He wanted the audience to know that he was prepared then or at any other time to put what he said to test. Manager Atkinson reiterated the condition of his bet, and said his $500 was then in the box office. He was sorry to say the city hall people had declined to put $250 into some charitable institution by failing and refusing to come to terms.

"Alderman Maginn said he had the money with him and was ready to bet it and go ahead with the performance. (Cries of 'put up or shut up.')

"Mr. Atkinson said that to arrange a bet before so large an audience, many of whom no doubt were opposed to betting under any conditions, was not the proper thing for him to do. He had been prepared to arrange the bet during all the day, and had tried to get them to terms, but no money had been put up against his, and it was too late, to say nothing of the indecorousness of it, to arrange a bet now. (This statement was received with cries, 'That's right.')

"Mr. Atkinson further stated that Alderman Maginn and his friends had better hire a hall, considering the advantage they had taken to back down in this matter. 'The little man' then left the stage amid hisses and cries of ' Lead him off! ' 'Put him out! ' etc.

"The tests with Miss Hurst continued. Mr. Cole and another gentleman then took hold of a billiard cue and tried to hold it, but failed. It flew over their heads and they could scarcely keep hold of it.

"The stage committee was then changed, and Dr. Smith, weighing 160 pounds, Dr. L. E. Leman, weight 230 pounds, Colonel Straight, weight 230 pounds, and Pap Lyman, of Leadville, weight 190 pounds, sat on a chair and were lifted from the stage by Miss Hurst placing one hand flat against the back of the chair.

"Mr. Atkinson said he had shaken hands with one of Miss Hurst's rivals during the evening and had found that it was stickey. He wanted Dr. Leman to examine Miss Hurst's hands and tell the audience whether they had any adhesive substance on them.

"Miss Hurst laughed at the ridiculousness of the idea, but held out her hand for the doctor to examine. He looked, and turning to the audience, said: 'Nothing but lily white.' This brought down the house.

"THE LITTLE MAN'S FAILURE."

"Manager Atkinson announced that 'the duplicators' of the performance would then be given an opportunity. Alderman Maginn ascended the stage, but the loudest cries for City Clerk Speer failed to bring him to the front. A dozen men sprang to the stage.

"Mr. Atkinson said he wanted fair play, and the audience must be the judge of the relative positions of Miss Hurst and her rivals while lifting a heavy man in a chair.

That was the one test which he desired her rivals to perform. He acknowledged that *one man could push another* about with a billiard cue against his breast.

"Then a light weight young fellow seated himself in a chair, and Alderman Maginn pushed up his coat sleeve and grasped the rim of the chair bottom like a vise. This called forth the loudest cries of denunciation from the audience and Miss Hurst's friends on the stage. They said Miss Hurst had not grasped the chair, but had simply placed her palms against it. The Alderman tried that and placing his left shoulder against the back of the individual in the chair, prepared for a mighty upheaval. Of course the man and the chair were rudely lifted. The audience hooted and yelled and laughed. Miss Hurst's friends on the stage and in the audience demanded that the same gentleman, whom Miss Hurst lifted, should occupy the chair, and be lifted in the same way. Dr. Smith took the chair and told the audience he was sitting in exactly the same position as when lifted by Miss Hurst. Mr. Maginn again placed his shoulder against the chair back and boosted for all he was worth. The chair lifted. Dr. Smith was indignant. He said anybody could lift the chair that way. Miss Hurst had not taken any such advantage. Mr. Maginn looked abashed and Dr. Smith kept up a terrible scolding. . . . . . .

"Alderman Maginn persisted in grasping the chair back and using his shoulder as a leverage. When the committee insisted on his doing as Miss Hurst had done, he failed utterly. . . . . . .

"'The little man' was frustrated at every point. The audience was overwhelmingly against him, and it was universally conceded that Miss Hurst had come off decidedly victorious."

Every paper in the city the next morning derided the puerile imitation of the power put upon the stage by these people.

Our challenge was renewed and our $500 kept in the box office, but in vain,—the $250 to be put up against it was never forthcoming.

CHAPTER XXIII.

"BOGUS LULU HURSTS SPRING UP OVER THE COUNTRY."

"Lulu Hurst's Double—A Deceitful Manager Exposed— The Georgia Wonder Resting at her Southern Home— D. H. P—— Tries to Play a Snap on the Detroit Public—It Will not Work."—Head-lines from the Detroit Times Article.

My great fame had the effect of producing a number of "bogus Lulu Hursts." They attached themselves to my name like parasites, to feed upon my reputation. I will let the Detroit *Times* tell of one of these impostors, which it does in an article under the head-lines given at the beginning of this chapter. The impostor's name was given in full, but I will only give his initials, as I prefer not to cause any offense to any one.

The article is as follows :

"About 11 o'clock yesterday forenoon the door of the city department of the *Times* was darkened by a dapper little gentleman, who introduced himself as D. H. P——, manager of the Georgia Wonder, Lulu Hurst, who had been announced to appear at White's Theatre this evening.

"Addressing the city editor, he said: 'I understand some doubts have been expressed by the *Times* concerning the identity of Lulu Hurst, who appears here under my management Sunday evening. Have you heard any such rumors?'

"'The *Times* has not learned of such rumors, though information it has received would lead to certain conclusions not altogether compatible with your announcement,' was the reply.

"'Upon what are they based?' inquired the manager, apparently laboring under considerable embarrassment, more or less suppressed.

"'On dispatches published in certain papers which call in question the identity of a person who has been traveling through Ohio as Lulu Hurst.'

"'One of them is from Warren, O., to the Cleveland *Leader*, and in substance charges that Lulu Hurst was billed to appear at the opera-house in that city, and that the manager on investigation found that this person so billed was not in reality the Georgia Wonder and pronounced her a fraud, refusing to allow the performance to be given.

"'Following is the dispatch:

"'Special dispatch to the *Leader*,—

"'Warren, Aug. 28.

"'For the past week big posters in heavy black type have announced that Lulu Hurst, the Georgia Wonder would electrify a Warren audience at the opera-house. The same parties appeared at the academy in Cleveland on Sunday night last, and Monday's *Leader* gave anything but a favorable criticism. When the handsome young man

who does the advance and treasury business for the Wonder reached here to-day Manager Lamb of the opera-house,
took him to one side and said to him : 'It's no use; the
people here are on to you ; you're a fraud.'

" 'The young man's subsequent movements were of an
active businesslike character. He paid his hotel bill and
inquired the nearest route to a train to Cleveland. The
Miss Hurst looked so strikingly like the manager that a
man who never saw them before said they must be brother
and sister, and the young man's name is not Hurst. The
opera-house manager denounced in no mild terms the
whole proceeding, and said that, although out of pocket for
advertising, he preferred to keep the doors closed rather
than defraud an audience. Meanwhile if the original
Lulu Hurst comes this way she will do a big business.'

"The above dispatch was not shown to the visitor, whose
confusion, however, seemed to increase.

"The following dispatch and extract, also in hands of
city editor, were alluded to but not shown the disconcerted
caller:

" 'Special to the New York *World*,—

" '"Chattanooga, Aug. 26.

" 'Lulu Hurst, the Georgia Wonder, was interviewed by
your correspondent to-day as she passed through the city
en route home. She will be under the management of
Chas. Frohman of the Madison Square Theatre, New
York, next season, which commences in San Francisco on
September 8th, and continues four weeks.'

"From the Boston *Herald*, Aug. 24.

" 'Lulu Hurst, in the course of the next two weeks,
takes a flying trip to the Pacific Coast for the purpose of

giving ten performances. She is paid for this trip at the rate of $1,000 per night. Two of the entertainments will be given in the Tabernacle in San Francisco, a place which holds about 5,000 people. The other performances will be given in the surrounding towns, and Miss Lulu Hurst will then come back to Chicago, resuming her tour of the Eastern States.

" 'She is at present taking a rest, having worked pretty hard for the past few months.'

"In answer to the allusion made to the above dispatch, Mr. P—— acknowledged that he had played at Cleveland, Youngstown and Canton, and produced a paper published at the above mentioned place giving a report of the performance. He denied that he had been in Warren; and in answer to further interrogation as to whether he had billed Warren, said with considerable emphasis 'No.'

"He was asked the whereabouts of Mr. P. M. Atkinson, Miss Hurst's previous manager, and said:

" 'Mr. Atkinson's contract with Miss Hurst has expired, and he has gone South to his home where he has other interests to look after.'

" 'Is Lulu Hurst under your sole management?'

" 'No, I have a backer,' with considerable hesitancy.

" 'Has Mr. Chas. Frohman anything to do with her management?'

" 'No.'

"The interview was at this interesting moment interrupted, and the young gentleman departed, considerably disconcerted.

"Following his departure, the following dispatch was sent by the *Times* to Chas. Frohman, Madison Square, New York City:

"'Lulu Hurst is announced here for Sunday evening. Is she *bona fide*?   P——, the name of the manager.

"'THE TIMES.'

"A reporter was also dispatched to ascertain the stopping place of Mr. P——, and to obtain an interview with the alleged Lulu Hurst.

"A visit to the Michigan Exchange, and an inspection of the Register disclosed the name of Miss Emma P. and D. H. P.   The former could not be found; the latter was again seen and in reply to further questioning maintained that he was the manager of the original and only Lulu Hurst.   He also stated that the lady with him was his sister, and that the Georgia Wonder was yet in Cleveland, but would probably arrive in the evening.

"When asked to account for the conflicting reports of Lulu Hurst's engagement for September 8th, Mr. P. professed to disbelieve the reports in the possession of the *Times*, and maintained that the other was not the genuine Wonder.   At the same time he failed to establish the identity of his own attraction.

"The *Times* by investigation in another channel ascertained that D. H. P. had for a short time been a clerk at the Michigan Exchange and that he had a wife who gave spiritualistic performances under the name of Annie Fay; also that he had several sisters.

"Later in the day the following dispatch was received at the *Times* office:

"'NEW YORK, Aug. 30, 1884.

"'*Editor Detroit Times*:

"'The genuine Lulu Hurst is in Atlanta resting for trip to California in September.   CHAS. FROHAM.'

"Upon receipt of the above dispatch an effort was made to see Mr. P. . . . He was not found, but about midnight the much-sought-for individual again entered the *Times* office, apparently considerably worried. He was invited to take a seat. To reassure him the following question was hurled:

" 'Is the lady stopping with you at the Exchange your sister or your wife?'

" 'She's my sister,' he replied.

" 'Are you a married man?'

" 'No,' was the rejoinder, accompanied by an inquiring look.

"The dispatches and extracts above given, were then read and shown to him for the first time. During the reading of them great beads of sweat began to stand out upon the visitor's brow, and the distress so plainly displayed was intensified by the assurance of the *Times* that his replies did not accord with other information in the possession of the paper. Drawing his chair close to his inquisitor, he said: 'I replied too hastily to your question awhile ago. I am a married man. That is her picture!' and he produced a card photograph disclosing a woman in flowing robes, with long hair streaming down her shoulders and back as she leaned forward in a somewhat tragic attitude.

" ' Does she not give spiritualistic entertainments?'

" 'No—yes—here is a slip that shows the class of work she does.' Whereupon Mr. P. produced a printed slip which was, in substance, a report of a performance of a mediumistic character.

" ' Is the *Times* going to open up on me again in the morning?' inquired the much-entangled manager. 'I wish you wouldn't say anything about these dispatches. I don't know why Chas. Frohman should give me away unless it is because he is a big, powerful manager and I am only running a little side show.'

"Giving his chair another hitch and bringing himself in closer contact with the reportorial corkscrew, he continued:

" 'I will tell you all about it.   I have been played for a sucker, and am the only one who will lose by this.   It will knock me clean out.   It is not Lulu Hurst that I have with me.   I just considered that I had bought the right to use Lulu Hurst's name and have paid for it.   .   .   .   . I wouldn't have had this exposure to have happened for a thousand dollars.   I had big money ahead, and now it is all knocked into a cocked-hat.   How much will it cost to keep it out?   This will ruin everything.   Can't you keep it out?   Do, that's a good fellow, and come over and see me to-morrow.   I will make it pleasant for you.   Wait till you see the performance Sunday night.   If you give it away Sunday morning, why that will end it all!'

Further entreaties were cut short by the assurance that the *Times* would not do him *full justice*.   The *Times* fulfils its promise, and does Mr. P. justice.

The following is from the New York *Times* and relates a funny thing that happened in St. Louis in connection with another bogus Lulu Hurst.

"Miss Lulu Hurst is said to have been met on Monday night by a very large audience in the Temple in San Francisco, a building capable of seating 5,000 people.   While this Georgia Wonder is appearing on the Pacific slope, a bogus Lulu Hurst, who used to give alleged spiritualistic seances in variety theaters, is masquerading in the less remote West. This ungenuine Lulu Hurst was recently announced to appear in St. Louis, but the local manager, discovering the fraud, refused to open his theater, and the agent of the Wonder promptly disappeared, thoughtlessly neglecting to pay his hotel bill. A few days ago the real Lulu Hurst, on her way to San Francisco, stopped in the same house, and the proprietor undertook to induce her to pay the obligation incurred by the agent of her counterfeit. The indignation of Miss Hurst, the rage of the worthy but excitable parents, and the withering scorn of Mr. Atkinson are said to have been worth a journey of 1,000 miles to observe. The bill was not paid."

The Atlanta *Constitution* of October 28th gave an extensive account of another bogus Lulu Hurst in a different section of the West, who at that time was attempting to "do up" Little Rock, Arkansas, and it seems was caught up with there. But I have quoted enough on this line to show the amount of weak counterfeiting that was going on over the country. It all goes to show how great was the fame at this time of the "Original Georgia Wonder."

CHAPTER XXIV.

FUNNY SCENES AND SAYINGS.

An Amusing Incident in Moberly, Mo., Illustrating the Credulity of Man—A Strange Request to Test Hypnotic Power.—"Her Power, Like Samson's, is in Her Hair."

I recall a funny incident which happened up in Moberly, Mo., which I think only goes to show the credulity of man.

There was an entertainment of some kind at the opera-house and we went to see it. Every one in the audience soon found out that Lulu Hurst was in the audience, even the theatrical people themselves, and towards the close of the entertainment a gentleman came out on the stage and made an announcement about like this:

"Ladies and gentlemen, you are doubtless aware that Miss Lulu Hurst will give one of her marvelous exhibitions on this stage to-morrow night. Of course you all will see her. She is indeed the Wonder of the nineteenth century. I saw her in New York, and she certainly gives the most wonderful exhibitions that I have ever witnessed. But while I am praising Miss Hurst, yet, ladies and gentlemen, I want you to understand that she is not the only person in the world who is the possessor of this wonderful power. Through my short interview with Miss Hurst in

New York, she very kindly revealed to me the secret of one of her wonderful feats, and I am going to give it to you here to-night."

So with this announcement he went to the wings of the stage and brought out a long rope. The audience was all excitement and interest. He tied one end of the rope to a post and then he tied a hard knot in the middle of the rope. He then took the other end and threw it out into the audience.

"Now," said he, "I want a number of gentlemen to come forward and take the end of that rope and hold it, and I will, by a process of will power, get that knot out of the rope without untying it from the post or without the gentlemen turning it loose."

Well, about six or eight gentlemen came up at once, and they just kept coming until there must have been twenty who had hold of that rope. Some of the best men of the town were there. About this time there seemed to be some little delay in the proceedings when one of the gentlemen holding the rope, asked:

"Why don't you go ahead? What are you waiting for?"

The fellow's reply was what caused the fun and collapse:

"Just keep quiet, friend, I am only waiting to see if I can't catch *one more sucker on this line.*"

At Danville, Illinois, after our entertainment had gotten well along, a gentleman rose up in the rear of the house and said:

"Mr. Manager, I have a request to ask of you, that I hope you will grant. It is this: I want you to ask the lady (referring to myself) *to speak a word to the audience.*"

My manager told him that he was paid to do the talking act, and that he didn't much like the idea of being thrown out of a job, yet, he had no doubt that I would gladly accede to his request, which I did by saying "that I didn't know what to talk about unless it be to thank the audience for their attention and applause."

Then my manager said to the gentleman:

"Now, sir, Miss Hurst has accommodated you, would you object to telling this audience your motive in asking her to speak a word."

His reply was quick and ready:

"Not in the least, sir. I have taken a great interest in Miss Hurst's power. I have kept up with her very closely. I felt quite sure that I could and would be able to solve the mystery should I ever be so fortunate as to see her. Well, when she began the exhibition to-night it was so entirely different from what I had expected, and was so far outside the pale of reason that all my preconceived theories were exploded at the outset, and the only solution I could see was, that it was possible, she was accomplishing these things while under a hypnotic spell, and that you were the hypnotist. But since hearing her speak I feel quite sure that this theory is wrong, and I frankly admit that I don't know as much about it as I did before I came here."

A lady at Vincennes, Indiana, exposed the whole thing by saying she knew what caused the Power; that she knew also how to stop it. My manager asked her what her solution was. Her reply was:

"*Cut off her hair. She gets her strength just like Samson got his, and she will lose it as he lost his.*"

And the credulous lady believed it.

CHAPTER XXV.

AN ILLUMINATION THAT DID NOT ILLUMINE.

A Panic Averted at Springfield, Illinois—A New and Most Remarkable Test—Chicago Outwitted and the Lynx-eyed Press Bewildered.

I could write chapter after chapter about our experiences in the West, but space forbids, and I must pass on. I do not want to make my narrative too long. I only want to put on record enough of my experiences to prove my case. I am not writing this volume simply as an autobiography and an explanation of my mysterious force, but also to teach some wonderful lessons in human nature and psychology. I want everything I say in Part II. of this volume to be immovably grounded on the facts and occurrences related in Part I. But I hope to avoid wearying the reader by a too lengthy recital of these remarkable events. It is a subject that can be very much lengthened out, and yet not unduly abbreviated. I find in it material that seems inexhaustible. Everything connected with the phenomena and myself from the beginning to the end makes a strange and almost inexplicable story, and a queer one to handle. Now in my maturer years, when I look back upon it all, and think how I as a girl got into doing these strange things, and how I caused all this continental commotion, it seems stranger than any fiction that ever came from the inspired imagination of a master genius.

From Denver we went to Pueblo, Colorado Springs and thence into "Bleeding Kansas," exhibiting in many of the important towns and cities. It was at Emporia, Kansas, that an amusing incident happened. Our exhibition was drawing to a close when a lady in the audience asked if I would speak a word to the audience. I did so, whereupon my manager said to the lady:

"Now, madam, Miss Hurst has granted your request, would you object to telling this audience why you wanted to hear Miss Hurst speak."

Her reply was prompt:

"No, indeed. I heard many strange stories in connection with Miss Hurst. I did not believe any of them until I came here to-night, but now after seeing her wonderful performance I am prepared to believe all that I have heard; and one of the strange things I have heard in connection with her was that when she spoke a brilliant illumination proceeded from her mouth, and I just wanted to see that illumination."

Unfortunately it was a bad night for fireworks and the illumination did not "materialize."

From Kansas we went into Missouri, Ohio, Illinois and Wisconsin. There was nothing that occurred out of the usual run of our entertainments except at Springfield, Ill. Here we came near having a serious panic in the opera-house. The house was packed, and we were in the midst of our entertaiment with the excitement attending the exhibition of the " Power" running at high tide.

Everybody was worked up to a high tension. Suddenly, amid the din and furor of excitement, a low, rumbling noise was heard. The house began to shake. The audience could not tell from whence this new phenomenon came. None could divine the cause of this alarming disturbance, yet they were ripe for anything, and in an instant the people were on their feet ready to rush for the door. When they were just on the verge of stampeding, my manager's presence of mind asserted itself just in time to avert a panic. He made a motion to the audience to keep quiet, and stepping to the footlights said:

"We will stop the exhibition long enough to allow all of the weak-minded portion of the audience to withdraw. Then we will begin the exhibition again."

Whether it was his calmness of manner or the fact that no one wanted to admit that they were weak-minded, that quelled the excitement, I know not. But the result was the panic was averted and the audience sat down again. The excitement was occasioned, we learned afterwards, by a heavy fire engine dashing over the rock pavement by the building on its mad rush to a fire. Ordinarily it would scarcely have been noticed, but the excited state of the minds of the audience was such (or appeared to be) that they did not take time to consider. They seemed to think the-whatever-it-was was there among them or on the stage, and that there was some impending danger attending it.

* * * * * * * * *

We soon found ourselves in Chicago, the queen city of the great northwest, where we exhibited to large crowds for ten nights in Central Music Hall. Sharp-witted Chicago succumbed to the "Invincible" as readily as the down-east or the southwest. The papers of this enterprising city were exceedingly liberal in writing up my performances. The great dailies gave column accounts, day after day, of all the phenomena attending the exhibition of the Power. In this city, what is known as my famous "Balance Test" caused a vast amount of consternation. I will describe it more in detail than I have heretofore done. It is done in this way: I stand erect on one foot and hold a billiard cue or strong stick in both hands in a horizontal position imme- diately in front of me, as shown in *figure 1*, PART II. Then I invite any one to stand on the opposite side of the object from me and push me backward off of my balance. This test always proved perfectly successful on my part, for no one, however strong, could by any amount of force cause me to move my position or lose my balance. When this wonder- ful discovery was made my manager wrote a full descrip- tion of it to one of the leading scientists at Washington, who had shown a deep interest in the "Power," and had requested us to keep him fully posted if any new develop- ments or tests occurred. His reply was couched in about the following words:

"If, as you say, Miss Lulu can stand erect on one foot and prevent me from pushing her off her balance, she is indeed a miracle."

The *Daily Inter-Ocean*, in one of its accounts, pronounces this "the most remarkable test," and says: "She endures the most remarkable test by standing on one foot and in a normal, perpendicular position resists the force of two men, who, pressing against a cue, seek to push her backward. It is impossible to move her."

This article says concerning the force:

"The tests, some of which have been described, are numerous, amusing and puzzling to the most skeptical. Her force does not seem to be in conformity with any laws of mechanics, unless, indeed, they be spiritual."

The *Herald*, in one of its comprehensive articles, says:

"It seems that magnetism is in some way connected with her inexplicable feats, which baffle alike the learned and the unpretentious. Her power is so formidable that one is thankful that her's is a peculiar gift and not a general endowment."

The *Daily Inter-Ocean*, in an editorial headed, "The Girl from Georgia," says:

"To ascribe Miss Lulu Hurst's peculiar powers to electricity is merely giving an old name to a new ignorance. Not a solitary accompaniment of electric excitement is present, and no mode of applying electricity ever yet scientifically brought to bear has produced any results bearing any resemblance to those witnessed in her case. The phenomena occur without regard to conducting and nonconducting substances, and the force, whatever it may be, does not pass from the chair or implement used by those who try to resist it. It communicates no shock to the persons resisting it, as electricity would. It is gradual and cumulative, and requires a very considerable time in each instance to gather the power, while electricity is instantaneous.

"Electricity in quantities that would kill a man has never heretofore been so applied as to directly lift two pounds. Lulu Hurst's force, on the contrary, apparently lifted in some of her experiments on Monday evening half a ton, yet had no power to shock a mouse electrically.

"It is no less useless to apply the term magnetism to experiments which lack all the qualities of magnetism and possess others which, magnetism would not account for.

"It is true that in the umbrella test the agitation among the wires and ribs of the umbrella, and the facility with which they seemed to break themselves to pieces at points where no visible force whatever was being brought to bear, indicate the presence of a sudden vibratory, mechanical agitation, transmitting itself with striking swiftness through all the umbrella, and which we would naturally attribute to Miss Hurst in some way, though she had touched only the rod of the umbrella and not the cloth or ribs. The agitation in the umbrella would be like that of the sails of a vessel suddenly demolished by a squall, and the umbrella would be 'knocked into a cocked-hat' with the same suddenness. But no man could produce the same results with magnetism or electricity applied according to scientific methods. It would be as scientific to say that Miss Hurst's power lies like that of Samson, in her hair, as to imagine that anything is explained by referring her power to magnetism or electricity."

The Chicago *Tribune* says in one of its long articles:

"The Georgia Wonder . . . . . . at least possesses the undisputed power of drawing large and cultured audiences. Women in beautiful costumes and men in full dress were plentiful at Central Music Hall last evening. Previous to her entertainment Miss Hurst, in the greenroom, received a score of the best people of the city, among whom were a number of interested women who took vast delight in examining her critically. * * *

"Among the large number of prominent citizens who

were on the stage during the evening were Messrs. Archie
Fisher, Arthur Caton, N. K. Fairbank and Mr. Clark, all
of whom tested the powers of Miss Hurst.

"Mr. Caton said: You might as well try to stop an
avalanche with a broom.' * * *

"Professor Swing, who had been a close observer of all
the phenomena, said: I am as much mystified as ever. I
examined Miss Hurst when it was all over, and she did not
appear to be tired or flurried.'

"Not a man who undertook to withstand Miss Hurst's
strange power could give any explanation of it."

The *Religio-Philosophical Journal*, in an exhaustive editorial, says:

"THE GEORGIA WONDER.

"Miss Lulu Hurst, of whom everybody has read, is
confounding the skeptical and silencing those who cried
humbug before seeing an exhibition of the tremendous and
mysterious power manifested through her while in a
passive state. * * *

"She is the wonder, the miracle of the century, astonishing and inexplicable."

The Chicago *Herald*, in a long editorial concerning the
Power, makes this remark:

"A traveler in California, after experiencing a first-class
shock of earthquake a few years ago, was found for the
next hour or two to be so dazed by the phenomenon as to
be unable to give utterance to any other word than the
single sentence, 'There is something about it that I don't
understand.' Those who witness Miss Hurst's performance are struck in much the same way. * * *

"She succeeded in proving to her audience that the

number of things the world cannot understand is increasing quite as rapidly as the area of its scientific knowledge."

I could fill a good-sized volume quoting from the Chicago papers alone, but must pass on. Our success there in every way was very satisfactory to us. The people were universally kind to us, and the papers exceedingly liberal and enterprising in writing about our performances.

From Chicago we went up to Milwaukee for a three nights' engagement. We opened our engagement with a complimentary performance for the press and leading citizens at the Plankinton Hotel. The *Sentinel*, in writing of this performance, headed its article thus:

"SHE PUZZLES EVERYBODY.

"*Lulu Hurst and the Power Behind the Thrown—The Georgia Wonder Entertained a Hundred Milwaukeeans at a Private Séance, and fairly Mystifies every One by Her Display of Unknown Power—Some of the Muscular Young Lady's Feats—Board of Trade Utterly Vanquished—Success of Different Tests.*"

"Mr. Peck, the editor of *Peck's Sun*, and the author of 'Peck's Bad Boy' (now Gov. Peck), was handled without gloves by the power at this performance. Mr. H. E. Rounds, of *Peck's Sun*, Capt. Dave Vance, Mr. J. B. Oliver, Postmaster Payne, Dr. Kaine of the *Sentinel*, and vast numbers of others went down in utter defeat before the Power."

*   *   *   *   *   *

The weather at this time was getting so very cold and disagreeable we decided to go southward. We came south, exhibiting in the towns and cities on our route, and finally terminated our tour at Knoxville, Tenn., where we gave two exhibitions to immense audiences.

At these, my last public performances, several hundred were turned away unable to gain entrance.

CHAPTER XXVI.

THE LAST THE PUBLIC EVER SAW OF "THE GREAT UNKNOWN."

Potent Reasons Why I Abandoned the Stage—A Fortune Laid at my Feet to no Avail—A Mysterious Resolution that Could not be Shaken.

At Knoxville, Tenn., was the last the world ever saw of "The Great Unknown." For after my second exhibition there, I decided to never give another performance. When I made this announcement to my parents and my manager they were dumfounded beyond expression. I had given them no warning of the determination which I had been forming in my mind for some time. When I made the annnouncement to them they laughed at me, thinking it was only one of my practical jokes which I was always so fond of playing on them and other people.. But when they did come to realize I was in earnest, they could not begin to express their astonishment. They seemed to think I was mad or going crazy, and began to reason with me. They asked my reasons for determining on such an unreasonable, uncalled for, unexpected, rash step, but I would give them no reasons.

They unfolded to me the alluring prospects before us,

how my fame had gone everywhere, how the people flocked
to see me by the thousands wherever I went, etc.

We had previously planned, and had large offers made us
for a tour through England and Europe, and they laid before me the pleasures and profit of such a trip as this.

. We had not covered more than one-tenth of the territory
in the United States, over whose immense borders my fame
was boundless, and they unfolded to me the vast money to
be taken in by continuing our exhibitions in this country.
The prospects were indeed bright, brighter than they could
possibly picture to me, and I knew it, yet I was immovable.
I listened to their entreaties with an unmoved will, and
heard their pleadings with an unaltered determination.

*   *   *   *   *   *.   *   *   *

And yet I gave them no reasons. But I had my reasons,
and I considered them all-sufficient. I would not express
them then, but I will now. The reader will see many of
them set out hereafter, but I will state a few of them here.

I had become burdened with the idea of the vast amount
of superstition and delusion in the public mind concerning
" The Power." From the time I left the city of Washington this burden had been growing heavier in my mind.
As my fame grew, the superstition of the people grew, and
the burden grew likewise. While I knew the " Power"
was wonderful and apparently inexplicable, yet I did not
like to be looked upon as some abnormal quasi-supernatural
sort of a being.

I despised any form of distinguished, famous, super-
normal isolation from other people. While I had always
repudiated the theories of "Spiritism," or "Psychism,"
and other such " isms" with which my "Force" had been

classed, yet I found it impossible to make the public do so.
The barriers of reason and natural law and order had been
set aside in trying to account for the "Phenomena" and
the public mind was like a ship at sea without a compass
or rudder.   Even then, as a sixteen-year-old girl, I realized
the harm to come to the human reason from thus trangress-
ing those eternally established barriers, which protect the
human mind from every form of invading superstition and
delusion.   I knew that every invasion of the fortress of
the human reason, of whatever form and pretext, weakened
its protective power, and rendered it an easier prey to each
succeeding superstition that came along.   I knew the spiritualists everywhere were pointing to me as the mighty
"Medium," though I always emphatically disclaimed such
an appellation.   While I could not then explain the nature
of the "Force," I always denounced such theories.   My
phenomena were beginning to be used to prop up all sorts
of outlandish and superstitious ideas and notions.   This
knowledge had oppressed me for a long time.

Well, I determined to stop, and never to give another
exhibition, and I never have from that day to this.   I said
to myself: If I can't explain this thing, I can at least hide
it and give the public mind a rest.

"The Great Unknown" and I can remain in mutual
isolation, and together fade from the public view.   And
in this solitude I will devote myself to the study of this
Phenomenon, and if I ever solve it so that I can demonstrate it scientifically to any thinking, reasoning mind, and
reduce it to the category of natural phenomena operating
along the line of cause and effect, then I will come before
the world with my explanation.   If I do not succeed in

this undertaking, I resolve to the day of my death to remain in the seclusion of my quiet home life, and carry with
me in solitude to my grave the mystery of
"THE GREAT UNKNOWN."

PART II.

THE EXPLANATION.

"The explanation as given makes the series of my phenomena, in some respects, the most wonderful of the century.

These phenomena are wonderful in more ways than one, and illustrate facts and truths and principles of human nature that will astonish the world more than I myself ever did when clothed in all the mystery of the Great Secret."

(From Part II., Chapter I.)

PART II.

CHAPTER I.

PREPARATIONS—SEARCH FOR THE TRUTH.

*A Few Principles Governing the "Power"—The Dawning
of Light in the Darkness.*

After I left the stage, for the reasons before stated, I determined to apply myself to the study of different branches of knowledge in order to acquire that knowledge necessary to prepare myself for life; also, having in view at all times the acquisition of such knowledge of physics and mechanics as would lead on toward an understanding and explanation of my "Power." I had already, before leaving the stage, gotten the idea that a part of the explanation was to be found in an *undiscovered or unrecognized principle of leverage applied in the* DEFLECTION OF FORCES. And as I began to think about it more and more, my wonder increased why some of the learned physicists had not discovered this principle while experimenting with me. I demonstrated it all the time without knowing it, and they did not detect it.

I attended one of the best and most thorough colleges in the country, the famous Shorter College, at Rome, Ga. By my school and college attendance I learned how to study. My mind was directed into channels of knowledge and taught how to investigate.

Afterwards I continued to apply myself, making use of the knowledge I had already obtained to go more thoroughly into those special subjects in which I was so deeply interested. Investigation into the principles of the lever and pulley was very interesting to me. I had to solve this point or problem in the study of my power:

COULD A CHILD FOURTEEN YEARS OF AGE, WITHOUT EXERCISING AN AMOUNT OF CONSCIOUS MUSCULAR POWER OR AGGRESSIVE FORCE AT ALL COMMENSURATE WITH THE UNRECKONED FORCE OPPOSING HER, BY SOME UNRECOGNIZED LAW OF PHYSICS, MECHANICS OR LEVERAGE, OVERCOME AND ANNIHILATE SUCH UNRECKONED AMOUNT OF MUSCULAR FORCE WHEN OPPOSED TO HER IN CERTAIN SPECIFIED WAYS AND POSITIONS?

As the years went by after I left the stage, and I studied the subject more deeply, I became more thoroughly convinced that in this question lay the kernel of the explanation of the majority of my feats. For I knew, and everybody knew, that had I exerted all the muscular force I was possessed of as a child, it would have been infinitesimal as compared with the tremendous forces brought against and opposing me. During my wonderful tests on the stage I often was compelled to exert what small muscular force I had as a child, but my exertion was so insignificant compared with the force I overcame that it never occurred to me then as worthy of consideration in the solution of the mysterious problem. I had settled one point while exhibiting on the stage, and that was this: *It was necessary for the force opposing me to exert itself by and through inanimate objects held in certain specified positions.* That was one of the first facts I specially observed even during the early part of my stage career. Why this was necessary I could not then understand, nor could I have given any reason for it. I also saw and recognized this principle: *That I had no power over inanimate objects unless in connection with opposing muscular force of another person. It was their exertion in connection with my influence that produced the phenomena.* The demonstration of each test will affirm and emphasize this principle, as we go into the explanation of them one by one.

Another fact I learned early in my career, which I can state here, was, that *the amount of the force opposed to me did not make much difference, except to increase the wonder of my performance.*

This may seem incredible to those not yet in the secret, but it is true. The truth is, I could often handle three or five men better than one. Professor Lafflin, of New York, the great athlete, and the renowned Japanese wrestler, Matsada, whom I met in Brooklyn, were of no more consequence to me than if they had been men of ordinary strength. I as quickly and utterly vanquished these giants of muscular strength and skill as I did the ordinary men experimenting with me; and if I used much muscular force it did not amount to anything as compared with their gigantic and stupendous power. The explanation will show that it was not necessary for me to exert but a minimum amount of muscular force.

The fact is, *I soon found out that the exertion of a large amount of muscular energy by my opponent or opponents in the tests was more of an aid to me than otherwise.* I will make this plain in demonstrating the tests, one by one, and it is important to keep this point in mind all the way through. *It was this principle that made my tests so wonderful.* Now, to be a little more explicit along certain lines, I want to explain what I meant when I spoke of not "exercising much conscious muscular power or offensive, aggressive force." I don't mean by this that I used *no* conscious muscular force at all, for it was necessary to use more or less force to keep my hand or hands in firm contact with the objects used in the tests, and often to give direction to the force in its beginning. But I mean that the muscular force used by me was as nothing compared with the force of those who opposed me in the tests.

I want to say further that often, in the excitement attending my public performances, I may have used a good deal of muscular force, and still not have been conscious of the exertion.

I know this, however, and so do all who witnessed my performances, that when I had baffled the muscular exertion of any number of strong men during a two hours' performance, and they would be, one after another, completely exhausted and covered with perspiration, I would appear and feel as fresh as when I started, and my pulse and respiration would indicate but a small amount of effort on my part. I used often to wonder at this myself, *but I understand now why it was not necessary for me to use any large appreciable amount of muscular effort. The explanation as given makes the series of my phenomena, in some respects, the most wonderful of the century. These phenomena are wonderful in more ways than one, and illustrate facts and truths and principles of human nature that will astonish the world more than I myself ever did when clothed in all the mystery of the great secret.*

I want to state FACT No. 1, which is this: *Every feat and " wonder," so-called, that I ever did was all the result of a little accident.* The first "rap" that was the beginning of everything, which occurred one night while my cousin, Miss Lora Wimberly, was in bed with me at our country home near Cedartown, Georgia, was the merest accident. It was this way (see the account in chapter 2, PART I): We were lying in bed resting and talking, and, in turning about, a hairpin in my hair was accidentally thrust through the strong feather ticking of the feather-pillow. This produced a very peculiar, loud, muffled, popping sound. Any one can try this, if they have the proper ticking, and see the effect. It was so sudden and unknown to both of us that we were both startled and frightened, as stated in chapter 2, PART I. But I soon discovered the cause of this peculiar popping sound; and being always of a very frolicsome, mischievous, pranking disposition, and loving fun and jokes intensely, I said to myself, "I will keep this and have some fun out of Cousin Lora." So then I used the hairpin, thrusting it into and through the feather ticking, and kept up the fun that night, thoroughly arousing the entire household. This started the excitement at home. I then found that by placing my feet in a certain way against the foot-board of the bed I could cause the wood to give out "raps" or popping sounds. This astonished me very much, for I could not then discover how this was done. But when I found that such a peculiar sound could be gotten that way from the wooden footboard, I kept this up to astonish the family and those about the bed, to amuse myself. I have since discovered the mechanical principles by which this was done, and how my famous "raps" from the table came, and, in fact, how all so-called "spirit table-rapping" is done.

. The placing of my feet against the foot-board of the bed and the production of those first raps were purely accidental, and I do not claim any credit for them. But in working out the problem since, and discovering how all " table-rapping " (called " spirit-rapping " by deluded people) is done, I have made a discovery that seems to me will be of untold value in ridding people's minds of the superstitions and delusions of "Spiritism" and of the impostors who thrive by these practices, under the garb of what is called "Spiritualism." Think of the thousands of people absolutely deluded on this subject and living all the time under the shadow of this great superstition!

From this simple, accidental starting point the wonders began and grew. The neighbors came in, and, as stated in chapter 2, PART I., we began *a test with a chair*, and I discovered the existence of this apparently inexplicable " Power " which then and there first manifested itself in *connection with me and* OTHER PEOPLE *when holding objects*. This accidental discovery confounded me, for I did not know and could not explain (being only a child then fourteen years old) how or why the phenomena occurred. The neighbors and friends there put forward the theory that it was some "unknown force" I was endowed with. I knew we had our hands on the chair and the people attempted to hold it, while it cut up wild and furious antics. But I noticed this was kept up by the excited people, even after I had *taken my hands off the chair.* This amazed me greatly. However, in these first experiments I *was quick to discover that no one or more of them could hold the chair when my hands were on it in certain positions.* And my wonderment and mystification increased when I saw excited, strong, sensible men, time and again tear a chair to pieces in their efforts to hold it when my hands were not upon it. And when they attributed to me the strange influence (which they claimed produced such phenomena) I was mystified, and my childish mind was led to accept this idea. I could not then have explained, to have saved my life, why this was so, but it is plain enough to me now, and I will demonstrate it when I explain the chair test.

Some people may wonder why I have waited all these years to make this explanation. It is a reasonable point of inquiry, I must confess. There are several very special reasons to account for my long silence. In the first place, I had and have no right to presume that the public would care much about having any explanation from me. I am going on a presumption in making one now with the expectation of the people taking much interest in it.

In the second place, I did not until recent years discover the principles underlying and governing the manifestation of this "Power," nor have I until recent years (when my judgment matured and my thought on this subject ripened) felt myself fully competent to *explain and demonstrate* my various tests as I desired to do. It has been, and is, my purpose to present this matter so forcibly and clearly, and make my demonstrations so complete, as to leave no possible room for doubt. To accomplish this has required time, study, thought, preparation.

Another cause that made me hesitate after making my discovery, was that I was afraid there might be persons cruel enough to charge my parents and manager with knowledge of, and complicity in, the performance of my feats. The fear of unjust criticism of them and not of myself has tended to keep me silent. *Of all people on the face of the habitable globe, they were the most conscientious believers in the occult nature of the Power.* Yet I was afraid I could not convince the public of this honest and candid truth. Not a member of my family ever knew that I had arrived at any "explanation" of the Power until two years ago, when I startled my husband by explaining to him the discovery I had made of the principle underlying the famous "Balance Test."

Now I want to state emphatically, Fact No. 2: That when the various tests of the "Power" developed themselves, when experiments were made with me at the time I was on the stage, *I did not know and could not have explained how or why the "Power" was manifested.* Except that, as I always made it a point to state, I did not have superstitious ideas about it, and ascribe it to "spirits," or anything of that sort.

Believing that I have now unraveled the whole mystery, and gone to the bottom of each of these remarkable tests, I propose to take them one by one and give an explanation and demonstration, so that any one can understand them, and ought to be able to perform them under the same conditions that I did.

I have introduced *illustrations* of each test I performed on the stage, so that I can demonstrate each one separately, and will now proceed chapter by chapter to do so.

One fact I will mention in conclusion : In my performances on the stage I had this advantage over any one now attempting the tests : There was then a mystery, a wonder, an "Unknown Force," that awed and mystified a great many people, and made them very susceptible to the "influence" of the Power. With this feeling gone it will appear very different to those testing it, and will take much of the excitement out of it. Hence sufficient allowance must be made for these changed conditions. This sentiment of mystery of dealing with the "unreal" and "unknown" was a very powerful factor in these tests. People came to test the "Power" prepared to believe anything and expecting anything. *These excited and* EXPECTANT *people* were the batteries and dynamos that generated much of the marvelous production which the public saw. This factor will be brought out in the demonstration of the tests as best I can, but it would be impossible to stress it as it ought to be.

CHAPTER II.

DEMONSTRATION No. 1.

" The Balance Test "—Pronounced One of My Most Remarkable Feats.

I have decided to give the demonstration of this test of my power first, because it was everywhere pronounced one of my "most remarkable feats," and the most inexplicable one, and because it was the first one that I discovered the explanation of, so that I could give a full demonstration of it. Though it was the last test of the Power, in point of time, put before the public, yet I give it precedence in the demonstration in order to show at the very beginning of the explanation how fully and completely the whole mystery can be demonstrated. I desire the public to be convinced at the very outset that I am not putting forth a mere unwarranted and groundless claim to be able to make a demonstration of all of my remarkable phenomena. This test was not introduced in my exhibitions until after I left New York city. Its discovery came to me by accident in this way: In experimenting with persons who were attempting to hold a billiard cue when my hands were upon it,

(212)

the cue was forced up, in their effort to hold it to a level
with my chest, I being on one side of the cue and the men
on the other.   In this position with myself standing perfectly erect and they pushing with all their might towards
me to keep from being hurled backwards by the force,
*I found that they did not and could not move me backward
off my feet.*

Their pressure exerted directly against and towards me
appeared to be annihilated.   Their combined pressure could
not sway me backwards an inch from my erect position.   It then flashed upon me in a moment that here was
a new test of my power!   We had for a long time desired
to get up some new method of exhibiting the force, and
my father had gone so far as to offer rewards to any one
who would suggest any new test of a feasible nature.
Well, after the exhibition that night I told my father and
my manager of my discovery, and, to prove it, I defied
them to push me off my balance when standing in an erect
position.   They struggled hard to do so, but could not
budge me.   I then told them I could stand on *one foot*
and they could not push me off my balance.   Strive as
they might they could not do it.   From this time on this
test proved a *"masterpiece of mystery."*   The investigators
and papers spoke of it as being "utterly inexplicable and
beyond the bounds of any trickery or muscular exertion."
I found that there were only two conditions necessary to
its complete success: One was that the experimenters should
push steadily and not spasmodically and jerkily.   The
other was that their pressure should be exerted in a direction *against* my body and not *upward toward or over my
head.*   Take the accompanying illustration *figure 1:*

I hold the cue *B A* out in front of my chest, grasping it at *D and C*, with the elbows bent at almost right angles, the experimenter taking the position as shown in the cut·

The cut shows only one person pushing against me; but more than one may exert their combined strength against me in this test. I request them to push as hard as they please directly against me, as shown by the line *E F*, and not upward toward my head, and to push steadily. Now you will observe their line of force begins at their feet, as a base, continues through the muscular system of the body, and passes along the arms and hands to the billiard cue. They necessarily strain and bend forward their bodies, as shown in the cut, in their efforts to push me, and this position naturally prevents their force from being exerted toward my head in the direction of the line *G H*, but tends rather to carry it horizontally toward my chest, and rather in a downward direction than upward. Now I want to state that before I discovered the explanation of my wonderful resisting force in this test, I recognized the general position of the parties and the direction of the force exerted by the experimenters, but I could not explain where the "great secret" of my "Power" came in *to annihilate such tremendous pressure as was brought to bear against me.*

So far as I could see, I exerted only enough resisting force to hold the billiard cue up and in place, and keep it from being pressed downward by the reclining weight and somewhat downward pressure of my opponent in the test. I supposed the "mysterious Force" was the bulwark that kept me from going over backward on my head. With the parties in the position shown in *figure 1*, no amount of pressure could push me off one foot. This I knew to be a

FIGURE I.

THE BALANCE TEST.

fact, indisputable and apparently inexplicable. Hundreds of learned men and trained investigators into the laws and phenomena of all known natural forces, critically made and observed this test, and pronounced it a mystery they could not solve. They saw the position of the parties and the direction of the exertion of their pressure just as well as, or better than, I did. They also saw and knew that standing perfectly erect on one foot with a billiard cue held out in front of me, that it was absolutely impossible for me to exert even 1-100 of the amount of muscular force that was brought to bear against me. Here were two or more powerful men, capable of exerting a pressure say, of 500 pounds or more, shoving with all the power of their mighty muscular strength directly against a billiard cue held in my hands, and there I stood on one foot unmoved, and apparently as immovable as a wall of granite.

Now, there could not possibly be but two explanations : Either all this force brought against me was annihilated in some unseen and inexplicable way, or I exerted a counteracting force equal to it. *That a girl standing on one foot, in an erect position, could push as hard as two strong men, was,* of course, too absurd an idea to be entertained for a moment. Then said these learned men and these lynx-eyed newspaper reporters all over the continent, this counteracting force of hers by which she accomplishes this wonder is of a "physic" or "odic" or "spiritualistic" character, or it is a "will force," that in some mysterious way is conducted along her nerves, and manifests itself in a form of muscular energy without the accompanying visible muscular exertion. The reader, who has read the first part of this book, has his mind full of all these mystifying explanations and superstitions which explain nothing, and are really as mysterious as the phenomena itself.

Now, I want to say right here, that when I began to really and earnestly study this subject with a view to making an explanation of it, I once and for all threw aside all such superstitious theories, kept strictly within the bounds of reason and common sense, and hewed squarely to the line of cause and effect. My mind is naturally neither credulous nor superstitious, but of a skeptical, close-reasoning nature.

I always believed that at the bottom of every fact and effect there must be a common sense cause, otherwise what *appears* to be a *fact* is nothing but an illusion or a delusion. This old world of ours needs to learn one great lesson, and to learn it well, and learn it forever, and practice it forever, that Nature has her eternal laws of cause and effect; that everything is and must be governed by them, that every *real, true fact* must be explained and understood by them when reduced to its last analysis; that anything which contradicts these laws is a snare and a delusion, and is neither a truth nor a fact, and that in every department of thought and knowledge these eternal laws of Nature and Reason are and must be supreme and immutable! He who engraves this supreme law on the tablets of his mind can never be a slave to superstition or a dupe to any form of delusion. The reader will pardon this little digression, but I could not suppress it as a protest against so much superstition in the minds of so many people.

Well, to return to the demonstration, here is the point I started at in my investigation, after throwing aside all these far-fetched and inexplicable explanations: I knew that I did not and could not exert 1-100 of the force that my op- ponents did, so I came to the conclusion *that I must have annihilated or dissipated their force in some way.   But how?*

Here was where the thought and work for me came in. I turned it over in my mind in every conceivable way.   I studied the subject of the lever, fulcrum, and pulley.   Fi- nally, one day, I said to myself, "When I find the real explanation of this thing, it is going to be very simple."   I threw aside all my books and asked myself, "Now, what is it I really do when this test is taking place?"   Nothing but exert enough force to keep that cue UP *in position, keep it from being pushed downward while I stand on one foot and keep my balance.   I thought this over and over, and over again.*

Finally, one night, in the early part of January, 1895, the scientific principle, the natural law that explained it perfectly, flashed into my mind!   I awoke my husband and cried out: "Eureka!   I have it!   I have solved it!" He was astounded at me, and asked me what I meant waking him up in that strange, excited way; that I had startled him very much.   I replied: "I don't care if I have; I have found out how that *balance test* is done.   It has just come into my mind like a flash.   You know I never had superstitious ideas about the "Power" like you had. Now I can explain *my most remarkable test,* so that you or anybody can do it as well as I can."   He said he did not believe me, and that I was simply joking him, as I often did.   But I noticed he eagerly asked me how it could be done, for he had always had the most far-fetched ideas about the "Power."   "Well," I said to him, "when I held on to that cue which those men were pushing with all their

might back *against* me, *by that little upward movement necessary to keep the cue in position, I deflected every bit of their
great pressure up into the air and off of myself!* I will tell
you the physical principle that is at the bottom of it : *It
is the Deflection of Forces,* and any one can do it." When
the strong men pushed that billiard cue back with all their
might and main against me, I had by the *slightest upward
pressure which was necessary to keep the cue in position,* AN-
NIHILATED *every bit of their force, and deflected it upwards
in the direction of the line G H in figure 1,* and thus, as it
were, dissipated it in the empty air. This same principle is
illustrated in the *glancing of a stone* when thrown with great
force, or of a rifle ball traveling with mighty speed, when they
strike an object ever so small and fragile at a tangent, or an
obtuse angle. A silk handkerchief or a small twig will
deflect a rifle ball from its course. A very thin sheet of ice
will deflect a swift-flying stone striking obliquely on its
surface. I had unconsciously applied this same principle of
glancing or deflection of force in this test. The force of
these powerful muscular men operating directly against me
in a horizontal direction, shown by the line *E F,* when it
came in contact with but an infinitesimal force at my hands,
exerted in a perpendicular direction, shown by the line *G H,*
was glanced or deflected upward into the air and annihilated,
so far as I was concerned, and affected me not in the
slightest. And yet out of the multitudes who saw the test
and experimented with it, not one ever recognized this simple principle of physics which, in one of its phases, is performed by every schoolboy each time he *skates a rock across
a pond covered with thin ice.*

FIGURE 2.

THE TEST OF ATTEMPTING TO FORCE A CANE OR BILLIARD CUE TO THE FLOOR
ACROSS MY OPEN PALM.

CHAPTER III.

DEMONSTRATION NO. 2.

The Test of Attempting to Force a Cane or Billiard Cue to the Floor Across my Open Palm.

This test was also one of the latest discovered by me. It was not introduced among my earlier feats. It was performed as shown in *figure 2*, as I will now describe :

The experimenter grasps the cue or cane *A B* at *E* and *F*, and I place my open palm flat against the under side and between his hands as shown in the cut at *C*. His hands at *E* and *F*, with the weight of his body and all of his muscular force exerted at these points, attempt to push the object *A B* in the direction shown to the floor. My hand at *C* never grasps the object, but only rests against or under it. This test was always a very mystifying one, and a great many absurd theories were advanced to account for

(219)

it. People sometimes said that I had a very adhesive substance of some kind on my hand to which the cane or cue adhered tenaciously. Often the doctors examined my hands to see if they could detect anything of this sort. When we exhibited in Denver and the "city hall crowd" led by Alderman Maginn, whom the papers there dubbed the "little man," attempted to duplicate my performances, it was discovered that some of them had their hands covered with an adhesive substance. My manager stated this fact to the audience, and asked one of the physicians present to examine my hands and state to the audience whether I had any such preparation on them. He did so, and stated that there was nothing there but "lilly white."

Other theorists said that my body was so intensely magnetic that its force caused an immense amount of attraction at the point where the cue or the cane came in contact with my hand. Some said that by a "prolongation of my will," I caused an invisible grasping of the object by unseen forces, which could not be overcome, or detected by the eye in the operation.

And so the various theories went on and on into the realms of superstition. I always knew that the pressure exerted by me at C in keeping my hands in firm contact with the object was but a minimum as compared with that exerted by the experimenters perpendicularly. I knew positively that I did not and could not *hold up or press upwards as much weight and force as these strong men could exert downward.* This everybody knew and admitted, but *what it was that counteracted all this downward pressure and weight was the puzzling question.*

What became of it? How did I dispose of it? In

what way could my open palm against the object annihilate it? It mystified me as it did everybody else when I
was on the stage, and I thought it over thousands of times.
After I had made the discovery of the principle by which
the "Balance Test" was performed, as explained in the last
chapter, I soon found that the same principle was the underlying explanation of this test. In this, the direction
of the force of my opponents was exerted directly downward, almost horizontally in a line of the object $A B$.
When this force was brought to bear on the object it necessarily pressed it in firm contact with my hand at C.
My effort was to keep up this contact at C and thus keep
my palm tightly pressed against the object. This simple
effort on my part brought into play the same principle of
"*Deflection of Force*," as was demostrated in the last chapter. Instead of the force exerted at E and F operating
down the line $A B$ towards the floor, it was deflected
at a tangent by my hand at C, and thus, by little
effort on my part, annihilated and dissipated, as it were,
into the air. The amount of muscular effort on my part
necessary to be applied at C to accomplish this feat,
was small, compared to the force expended by the experimenters at E and F. I have thus with no more pressure
than was essential to keep my hand in firm and rigid contact at C (and generally this small pressure was brought
about by the force from above pressing the object against
my hand, and not by any large amount of voluntary exertion on my part) prevented a force equal to 500 pounds
from carrying the object $A B$ to the floor. Instead of
this force from above continuing on in a straight line to
the floor and so carrying $A B$ with it, it was by a much

smaller amount of lateral pressure at C deflected in the
direction of $x\,y$; and so instead of the object $A\,B$ going
in a perpendicular course to the floor it persevered, in spite
of all the powers above, in going from the floor and in the
direction of $x\,y$. This deflection of the force of the experimenter rendered it necessary for him to constantly
keep changing the position of his body and his feet, in
order to get a purchase to keep up his pressure, and this
necessity to change, which he did not understand, kept
him excited and bewildered all the time. This, of course,
augmented in his mind the idea of mystery about the
"Power" which he already had, and this idea so firmly
fixed in the minds of my experimenters was always an
incalculable aid to me in overcoming and mystifying them.
As I view it now, this fixed idea of mystery was always an
aid and an advantage to me, which those will not have
who now do these feats, when this explanation has cleared
the mystery all away. But still, these heretofore unrecognized principles of the application of force, which I have
herein explained, will, if properly applied, as I have shown,
accomplish just what I have done hundreds and hundreds
of times before the most learned investigators of the continent—and which was never recognized by them.

When understood, it is very simple, just as was the
"Balance Test," and is exactly on the same principle as a
boy skating a rock on a thin coat of ice. He may hurl
the stone ever so hard and the coat of ice may be ever so
thin (so that even an infant's strength might break it),
yet, when the swiftly flying stone comes in contact with the
ice at a tangent, it glances off, is deflected away, and passes
on in an entirely different direction from that it was intended to take.

Just so with this experiment. The force applied along *A B* when it comes in contact with a slight pressure of the hand at *C*, glances off and carries the object in a different direction than towards the floor, and hence the result is that no amount of pressure applied can push the object to the floor.

CHAPTER IV.

DEMONSTRATION NO. 3.

The Heavy Weight Lifting Test.

This test was always and everywhere considered very remarkable, because of the enormous amount of weight which I lifted clear of the floor—six or more inches—by the placing of the palms of my hands against the back of the rear upright posts of the chair in which the weight rested.   I always disclaimed performing any of my tests by the medium of inanimate matter.   In this lifting test, as in the others, my force acted in conjunction with other animate beings—men and women.   The weight in the chair must always be men or women.   From the first time when I performed this feat, I was fully aware that I did not lift, and could not have lifted the six or eight hundred pounds in the chair (and I often lifted even more than this) by a mere exertion of muscular force; for I could not lift any more than any ordinary girl of my size.   I was not more muscular than other girls.   I did not understand, and could not explain upon what principle it was done, nor could learned men explain it.

FIGURE 3.

THE HEAVY WEIGHT LIFTING TEST.

They observed the fact that I did it, but could not explain how I did it, nor the mechanical principles underlying it. When this feat was tested by the scientists in Washington, in Prof. Bell's laboratory, as I have stated, they placed me on a pair of scales, and, after having ascertained my exact weight, they removed the pea up 20 pounds. I then stood on the scales and lifted a chair containing a man weighing 200 pounds without increasing my weight the 20-pound margin given. Now here appeared to be an annihilation of nearly 200 pounds of weight and nothing to account for it. If by my muscular force I had lifted the 200 pounds, then my weight on the scales must necessarily have been increased by the amount I lifted. But it was not increased the 20-pound margin given me to lift in. So the question was, what became of the weight when I lifted it? This answer no one ever gave, but I can now give it, and can explain it so that any one can perform it.

Now let us get clearly in our minds the exact position of the parties sitting in the chair, the position of the chair and my position in making the lift. It is all plain enough to me now, but what a mystery it used to be. The party takes his seat in the chair, see *figure 3*, and is requested to place his feet firmly on the floor at A and B, grasp the chair seat on each side as shown at D, and tilt the chair back so as to throw all his weight on the rear legs of the chair at G and H. I found out by experience that this was the position for me to make the lift in.

I at first thought, and it so appeared, that this was the

15 l

proper position to certainly throw all the weight on me when I lifted. Everybody seemed to think so too. It was also thought necessary to keep the feet in connection with the floor, in order to produce and sustain the "*current of the force*" by which it was believed the results were accomplished. For at the time I first began to perform this and other tests, everybody thought the Power was electric or magnetic.

Now when the first party had gotten in this position, a second large man was requested to sit in his lap or astraddle of his legs, and not allow his feet to touch the floor. Then a third man was requested to mount the shoulders of this one, as shown in cut. In this way and in these positions we have gotten an aggregate weight of 600 pounds in the chair—see the position in *figure 3*. I then placed my open palms against or behind the upper part of the rear post of the chair on each side, as shown at *C*, and made the lift without grasping the chair in the least. Now it would appear to any one who witnessed the feat, (1) either that I really lifted 600 pounds, muscularly, by the pressure of my palms, which was marvellous, or (2) that by some process this large weight was *annihilated*, which was miraculous; or that (3) I did it by some intangible, unseen, unknown force which was "occult," "spiritualistic," "psychic," "odic," or supernatural. This latter view was the one people took refuge in. When I began to study the problem in earnest, I threw away all three of these theories and investigated it on the line of the *the lever and the fulcrum*. In other words, *I postulated the theorem that it was to be accounted for on the principle of leverage, and went to work to prove it.* I have succeeded in *demonstrating* to my own satisfaction that this is the true solution, and I will now demonstrate it to my readers, so that they can perform it as I did.

Now let us remove all the sitters from the chair except the first one, who, we will assume, weighs 250 pounds. He takes the position as shown in *figure 3*, the chair tilted back, his feet firmly planted on the floor at *A* and *B*, and his hands grasping the chair on each side at *D*, and his body perfectly rigid. Now, in taking this position, *the man and the chair together constitute what I will term " a compound lever" with two fulcrums*—one at *A B*, and one at *G H*—the former fulcrum being at the further point of the lever formed by the man's feet, and the latter near the center of the lever formed by the rear legs of the chair. Now when the chair and the sitter are in this position, the entire weight is distributed at the two points designated as the " two fulcrums," the sitters' feet and the rear legs of the chair. Now I place my palms against the chair post, as shown at *C*, and, as I see it now, instead of *lifting* the chair the least bit, *I press these posts forward, and lo!* the chair with the entire weight comes up, leaving nothing touching the floor but the man's feet. Now when I pushed the chair post forward at *C*, what really took place? This little movement shifted all the weight from the fulcrum at *G H*, and threw it forward upon the fulcrum at *A B*, which really constitutes the point of the lever. The amount of the *push* at *C* necessary to do this is small, compared to the amount of weight which is apparently lifted.

Now let the other two men sit as described before, upon and astraddle the first sitter's legs, with their feet clear of the floor. Their weight will also be distributed at the two

fulcrums, as was the first man, but the most of it will
be thrown at *A B*, because in the effort of the first sitter to
keep himself and the chair in the proper tilted position,
the weight of the other men on his legs is necessarily sustained at his feet at *A B*. This additional weight upon the
first man's legs, instead of materially increasing the weight
thrown at *G H*, the second fulcrum, *tends to lessen* it there,
and throws it nearer the point of the lever at the man's
feet, and thus was an aid to me instead of an additional
weight. The parties being in this position, I push forward
at *C*, and lo! the 600 pounds and the chair rises six inches
from the floor. With the parties in this position the man
in the chair does most of the lifting, and I simply manipu-
late the compound lever composed of the chair back and
rear posts and the man's legs. Also what is known as the
principle of a Resultant Force comes into play in this test,
for when I push forward one lever at *C*, he is pushing backward at *A B*, and these two forces coming together create
a *resultant force*, operating in a perpendicular direction and
carrying the chair and its weight upward.

How fully this feat illustrates the axiom of the old philosopher who said that given "a place to stand on, a fulcrum and a lever long enough, he could move the earth."

From my best calculation (which I do not claim to be
mathematically accurate), I think that a pressure equal to
20 pounds, applied to the chair post on each side at *C*, will
raise a weight in the chair amounting to 500 pounds, if
applied under the same conditions that were used by me in
making this test. And I must say here that it is marvelous
to me now to think of the wonderful results I accomplished
in this and all my feats, without knowing anything about

the scientific and mechanical principles on which they were based. And in this statement everybody who saw my remarkable tests performed before large and critical audiences and committees must concur. All who saw me do these things were astounded beyond expression, and went away with all sorts of vague, occult theories in their minds about "how it was done."

CHAPTER V.

SOME REFLECTIONS BEARING UPON DEMON-STRATIONS, NOS. 4, 5, 6 AND 7.

DEMONSTRATION NO. 4—DEMONSTRATION NO. 5—DEMON-STRATION NO. 6—DEMONSTRATION NO. 7.

In the description and explanation of the tests which are now to follow, there are several more elements and forces that enter into them than concerned the preceding ones, which I have demonstrated. These elements and forces are so complicated and far-reaching, so remarkable and psychological, that they will be more difficult to demonstrate to the reader's comprehension if not to his satisfaction.

The tests now to be considered are :

1st. "The Umbrella Test," the attempt of the experimenter to hold an open umbrella above his head by grasping the handle with both of his hands, while I place my open palm against the handle between them.

2d. The attempt to hold a billiard cue or cane or chair, the experimenter to grasp them firmly with both hands, hold them steady, and stand still when I place my hands upon these objects.

3d. The attempt to force a chair to the floor, when held by the experimenter, with my hand or hands upon it.

Each one of these tests will be taken up and illustrations given, showing the positions of the object, the experimenter and myself, when making the test, and a demonstration will be given of each, showing fully and exactly the part taken by me in the performance of these truly wonderful feats, which so astonished the world.

But before going into these demonstrations, I want to state some facts and make some observations, which apply alike to all of these tests. *This concerns the part played by the public, the experimenters themselves, in the production of such remarkable results as took place.* It may be difficult for a person sitting calmly down reading this account, to realize or comprehend, the full weight and significance of what I am going to state, but it is every word the truth, and just as these things took place on the stage, and as the facts appear to me after having studied them faithfully and calmly for years. Now I want to state positively, *that the people, who came on the stage, as subjects, to take part in these tests, unconsciously performed a large part of what was done, made a considerable part of the exhibition, and furnished the greatest cause of all the wonder, merriment and fun.* As I see it now, the force put in motion by me simply provided the starting point—furnished the pivot—as it were, for them to revolve upon, and they did the rest. Now I can give my conjectures and my conclusions as to what made them act as they did in these special tests, and the reader can accept them if he wishes, or he may form conclusions of his own about it, if he can find any more satisfactory to his mind than those I give. And I am convinced that what I am going to state is the solution and the only solution.

In demonstrations Nos. 1, 2 and 3, heretofore given, I was the *passive* agent, as it were, in performing those tests, though, at the time, I did not comprehend what part I performed. In these tests the experimenters exerted their forces and weight against me, which I, or the "Unknown Power," had to resist, and then overcome.

But in the three under consideration now, the people experimenting with me were themselves the *active agents*, though 'they did not comprehend at the time that they were.

In the former three they simply furnished me a starting point or pivot or momentum of action, and in these latter three I merely provided it for them.

Now what caused the people to do these strange things on the stage, and at the same time left them with the firm conviction that the wonderful amount of force exerted, the extraordinary manifestation produced, were all caused by me? Well, in my opinion, there were several factors that entered into the production of this enigma. The first and foremost of these was the *superstition* of the people. This word conveys the idea pure and simple and unadulterated. I put a great many occurrences and facts and newspaper accounts in PART I of this book, to bring out and illustrate this point.

In viewing and thinking about the phenomena connected with the Power, which they saw and read most wonderful accounts about, the people abandoned the dictates of reason, forgot all common sense laws of cause and effect, and filled their minds with delusive theories and hocus-pocus ideas. They came to my tests with a pall of mystery draped over their minds, and their thoughts and faculties shackled with a *blind expectancy and anticipation that some weird, occult,*

*wonderful force was to take possession of them, and cause them
to do my bidding!* This idea was dominant in the minds
of nine tenths of my subjects. Their state resembled closely,
if it did not quite approach, what is known as "Hypnotism
by Auto-Suggestion." For I did not consciously attempt
to hypnotize anybody. At that time, as a mere child, I
knew absolutely nothing about hypnotism. I had never
seen nor read of an instance of it, and yet, from what I know
of its phenomena now, vast numbers of my experimenters
acted exactly like hypnotic subjects do. So they must have
been under the complete domination of "Auto-Suggestion."
In other words, to put it plainly, their blind, delusive expectation of what was to happen, took such complete possession of their minds as to render them obedient, though
unconscious, agents in doing to perfection what they expected would take place.

There are no series of incidents and examples in all the
history of hypnotic phenomena which—in multiplicity,
range, nature of absolute control, occurring for over two
years, covering a whole continent, affecting the learned
and ignorant, the savant and the ignoramus, the phlegmatic
and the neurotic temperament alike—approach in magni-
tude the phenomena attending my exhibitions extending for
a period of over two years in all parts of this country. It
is to my mind a psychological problem of vast importance.
It shows the absolute sway of the imagination over all the
faculties and mental and physical powers of the human being, and in this case it illustrates it on such a stupendous
scale!

It has caused me to stand aghast ten thousand times at the
absolute credulity and susceptibility of mankind! It has led

me to ask myself times without number, what are the opinions and statements of people worth on certain lines of thought, theory and belief? Let any one read the record furnished by this book and draw the conclusions for himself.

During my exhibitions when I would see the strange ways people acted, each in a different manner from the other, I would be overwhelmingly astounded and intensely amused. No wonder I laughed so much and won the appellation of "Laughing Lulu Hurst."

To say that I, a girl of immature mind and will power, hypnotized these people, as many authorities asserted, and made them act in these strange ways, is absurd, for I did not know how they were going to act any more than the audience did.

It is no wonder my audiences, as well as myself, were always so convulsed and uproarous in their merriment, when they saw their friends, acquaintances, townsmen and neighbors acting in so many different, funny and ludicrous ways.

Now to say that when all this was going on, I, the girl, who was the innocent cause of it all, knew what did it and what made people do this way, and that this girl was really the *efficient* cause of it all, is to me ridiculous and beyond belief. I then knew no more about it and was no more the *efficient* cause of it, than anybody else in the audience. I was simply the medium or *motif* that led to it.

People got up the notion, and article after article was written to this effect, that the peculiar " Force " or " Influence " I was supposed to be endowed with, acted upon or through *inanimate* matter; and I was compared with various "witches" and "wizards" and "occult prodigies," ancient

and modern, who were alleged to have such and such powers,
etc. The real common-sense truth is, they had no such
"Powers" over inanimate matter any more than I had, nor I,
any more than they, and the belief of such things is delusion
and superstition pure and simple. We see certain facts we
cannot at the time understand, or hear such and such statements and opinions from apparently credible and reliable
sources, which, under the circumstances and environments,
as related (mark the words) appear inexplicable and out of
the natural order of cause and effect; and straightway our
minds are flooded with a deluge of so-called supernatural
occurrences and facts, which are constantly added to by
each narrator—and then follow the "theorists," the "ideal-
ists," the "occultists," the "spiritists," the "theosophists,"
the "psychists," *et id omne genus*!

There may be some people who will consider my words
harsh and too sweeping and emphatic, but I have had experience enough on this line to have a common-sense opinion about these things, and, if the public will pardon me,
to throw out the admonitions scattered along through this
volume.

People should learn to never depart from the guidance
of reason in all things, and to never abandon in their in-
tellects the truth of the universal rule, *both as to time and
space, to period and place*, of the eternal laws of cause and
effect. These precepts alone will shield the mind from
its enslavement to delusion, ignorance and superstition.
Whoever departs from these will find himself led by will-
o'-the-wisps into deep, dark forests and dangerous quag-
mires, and he will eventually become lost from the guidance of reason and the protection of common sense.

DEMONSTRATION NO 4.

THE ATTEMPT OF ONE, TWO, THREE, OR MORE MEN TO FORCE A CHAIR TO THE FLOOR WHILE MY HANDS ARE UPON IT.

Now bearing in mind the emphatic statements I have made as to the part the public played in these tests, we will take up Demonstration No. 4. To get the positions of the parties to this test clearly outlined in the mind see the accompanying cut, *figure 4*.

The man *A* is requested to grasp the chair *B* firmly and press it to his breast and keep it there. He is instructed to attempt to put this chair to the floor when I (represented on cut by *C*) place my hands upon it, as shown in *figure 4*. Now, without an exception, when my experimenters attempted this test they had the idea fixed in their mind that they had to hold the chair with an intense pressure to their bodies, to guard against any danger from the force causing it to fly off. The truth is, in all my tests it *was* necessary for objects to be so held, as experience had taught us on numerous occasions, and as the record in PART I. conclusively shows.

This manner of holding these objects caused their whole body to become perfectly stiff and rigid. Their legs were exactly like stilts, and their backbone like a shaft of iron. Even their muscles were rendered untrustworthy, inflexible and almost impotent by the tension put upon them, in the cramped and strained position the man had assumed to protect me and himself, and resist the force. As he stands there firmly hugging that chair, he has no more suppleness in his limbs and body than a post, and he is just as easily pushed off his balance as is a post standing on end.

FIGURE 4.

THE ATTEMPT OF ONE, TWO, THREE OR MORE MEN TO FORCE A CHAIR TO
THE FLOOR WHILE MY HANDS ARE UPON IT.

Well, he has instructions to put the chair to the floor, and at the same time he must hold the chair firmly to his body. He can't put the chair down without releasing it from his tight embrace and limbering up his backbone, his legs and his muscles; this he never thinks of doing, or if he thought of it, he dare not do it, for he is afraid of the danger from the strange action of the " Force " if the chair gets away from his firm control. Suppose he relaxes himself enough to start the chair downward, the gentlest pressure from my hands on the chair, *which is a most potent lever in the position in which it is held*, causes this *human post* to lose his balance; and the least effort he makes to get on his feet steadily, and regain his balance, causes him to lift the chair upward instead of putting it any further downward.

Now I state that the amount of effort required in this test and struggle, to keep my hand in a positive and firm contact with the chair is about all the push that is necessary to keep this man off of his balance, so that he can never put the chair to the floor. Instead of his force being expended in a downward pressure on the chair as he thinks it is, it is all consumed in two processes, which he is really unconscious of. The first is the constant effort to keep his balance. The second is the subjective strain he has put upon himself to stand firm and hold the chair to his body—this strain being very great and consuming a large amount of the muscular energy expended by him. He is largely controlled in doing these things by his superstition and his imagination. He imagines he is to contend with an unseen, unknown enemy, and he must brace himself against it. This is his idea. He is like a man trying to run and at the same time is compelled to keep looking back to watch for his approaching enemy. He is sure to fall.

Well, when the man has tried and tried, and the chair does not go to the floor, we call in others to assist him, shown in *figure 4 as D and E.* It makes no difference how many come into the test, the result is the same. *In spite of all they can do, these men will work against one another and keep the chair up!* I have time and again, stood to one side *without touching the chair*, and seen a half dozen men tear it to pieces in their efforts to put it to the floor, and never succeed. In spite of all they could do, they would oppose their force against one another, and some would be pushing down and some lifting up, and others shoving to one side, and the result would be the chair would never go down, but more than likely be torn to pieces.

As I see it now in the light of this explanation, even when all these men were tussling, when my hand was on the chair, I did by the exertion of the little force used, keep them thrown off their balance all the time, and instead of forcing the chair to the floor, they were kept busy trying to keep their balance and stay on their feet. I never realized until recently what a small amount of force it takes to throw a man, or a number of men, off their balance when their muscles and their bodies are in a state of tension, especially, when one has the amount of leverage that I now see was always furnished me by the chair. The force they exert in this state *is all pent-up in themselves*, instead of being opposed to me; and they are as easily toppled over (with the *purchase* furnished by the chair and their stiffened arms and bodies as a lever) as a stick of wood on end.

At the time I was performing these feats, I did not comprehend these principles, nor could I divine what caused these men to do these strange things. I knew absolutely and positively that I did not, and could not, exert the *amount of muscular force* necessary to accomplish such results, for frequently I was not touching the chair. At every one of my performances, it was astonishing to me to see how strong men struggled with these inanimate objects and wrestled with one another.

The nearest approach to an explanation of these remarkable phenomena that I have ever seen in print I read in the *Medical Record*. Drs. Jordan, Terry and Grimes, of Columbus, Georgia, had written several articles concerning the "Wonderful Power," giving in detail the phenomena produced by it. In commenting on these articles the editor wrote, in addition to many other things, these lines:

"We fully believe that Dr. Jordan has described the phenomena correctly, and that Miss Hurst is a remarkable girl. But there is one feature in all her performances which no one, not even Dr. Jordan, seems to have noticed, or, at all events, carefully studied. This is, that all the exhibitions of her wonderful force are exhibited in opposing voluntary muscular effort in others.

"This force has no power over dead matter, but only over living, conscious, muscular exertions. This fact explains, we believe, the mysterious energy which the Georgia Phenomenon appears to develop.

"*It is the experimenters, not the subject, who knock themselves, the chairs, canes, umbrellas, etc., about. At any rate the matter ought to be investigated from this standpoint. It will probably be found that Miss Hurst's exhibitions are only another phase of the hypnotic phenomena.*"

The first experiment ever given of this test mystified me beyond expression. After the struggle began to put the chair to the floor, I stood to one side without touching it, and saw six excited, struggling men tear the chair to pieces without ever forcing it to the floor, all believing that the "Great Unknown" was keeping it up.

The accomplishment of this test then was based upon:

(1) The excited state of the subjects themselves, their superstition and their imagination taking such complete possession of them as to produce a state of partial self-hypnotism.

(2) The position of their bodies, limbs and muscles, in holding the chair and attempting to put it to the floor, was so strained and tensed and warped, as to render them largely incapable of exerting their force in the direction intended.

(3) With the position of the body and limbs, and with the chair as a powerful lever, it required but little exertion to keep them off their balance, and in a constant effort to regain it, so that, their force was all expended in this way instead of forcing the chair downward, and also, in their excited state, they expended their force largely in contending against one another.

(4) I see now that by this small exertion on my part, with the aid of this lever, *I constantly deflected their force, and instead of it operating downward, it operated laterally and was lost.*

FIGURE 5.

THE UMBRELLA TEST.

DEMONSTRATION NO. 5.

"THE UMBRELLA TEST."

The same Principles Discussed in the last Demonstration Apply to this Test. Here the Application of those Principles is a little Different, and the Object to be Accomplished is Different.

An umbrella is opened as shown in *figure No. 5.* The experimenter and I stand under it, and the former grasps the handle firmly at A and B, and I place my hand against it at C. He is requested to stand firmly and hold the umbrella, when I place my hand on the handle at C. The result of the performance of this test, as shown so often in PART I of this book, was always remarkable and extremely ludicrous. Within a few moments after my hand came in contact with the handle at C, the experimenter would lose his balance, and then begin to totter about trying to regain it. He would soon begin to gyrate about at a terrible rate. The umbrella would take on his motions, and its momentum and the force of the air beneath its folds would accelerate these wild contortions. The umbrella would become fierce and furious in its airy gyrations. Woe be to him who came too near it! as many people can testify who received wounds from its numerous beaks. It would act like a great, enraged vulture of some kind, who was trying to attack everybody within its reach. Its motions were swifter, more buoyant and airy and harder to control than those of other objects experimented with.

This test generally ended up with the experimenter losing all control of himself, the umbrella being jerked to pieces or turned inside out by him and the force of the imprisoned air beneath its folds, and all going down in a heap upon the floor.

16 1

Now what did I do? what part did I play in this extraordinary performance when I placed my hand upon the umbrella handle at *C?* As I see it now, I did nothing whatever, except to maintain *a firm contact at C, release my contact somewhat when I felt the experimenter pushing, and increase it when I felt him give way in the other direction,* at the time believing that it was the action of the "Force" which I was following up. The gyrating, buoyant motion of the umbrella kept the dance going at a lively rate when it once got started. All I did was to try to keep up with the time. Of course the experimenter, the audience and myself thought the "Unknown Force" was doing it all. The truth is, the experimenter himself was the "Unknown Force." By the least amount of pressure on my part, *in my effort to keep up with him,* he was constantly kept off his balance, and frequently when my hand became disengaged from the umbrella he would keep np his gyrations.

As it now appears, the position of the man's arms and the umbrella *extended and distended as they were, gave me a powerful lever,* which, with but a minimum amount of force on my part, furnished the starting point for the accomplishment of these most astounding results. The mystery surrounding the whole subject, as viewed by everybody, added immeasurably to my wonderful success. On account of this mystification the experimenters very quickly lost all presence of mind and all self-control.

This remarkable "Umbrella Test" was accomplished upon three principles :

(1) The mystery and the expectancy in the mind of the experimenter, which made him an easy victim.

(2) The wonderful *leverage* which I discovered and applied without knowing its action. And

(3) *The losing of his balance caused by the tensed and strained position of his limbs, muscles and body, and the remarkable purchase I had on him by reason of his position and the leverage given me.* All I ever had to do to accomplish this test was to apply and then relax a gradual, imperceptible pressure at C, until the experimenter lost his balance, and then keep up the contact at C as best I could, in my efforts to keep up with him. The pressure that I exerted was not noticeable. In the anxiety and expectancy of waiting for the oncoming of the "Force," which was frequently delayed, my muscles must have exerted a sufficient gradually increasing force to accomplish the result.

The truly wonderful manifestations which the applications of these principles produced, and the effect upon the public, can be but partially and meagerly realized from a reading of PART I of this volume.

DEMONSTRATION NO. 6—DEMONSTRATION NO. 7.

THE ATTEMPT TO HOLD A BILLIARD CUE, A CANE OR A CHAIR, OR OTHER LIKE OBJECT, WITH MY HAND OR HANDS ON THEM.

These tests all involve the same principles, and will be demonstrated together. They are also so closely allied to "The Umbrella Test" that the same observations made with reference to that apply to these. These are controlled by the same mechanical principles as that.

The position of the parties in making these tests are shown in *figures 6 and 7.*

The positions in holding the cue or cane is shown in *figure 6.* And that in holding the chair in *figure 7.*

In these positions the experimenter (or experimenters, for several may take part in the tests) was required to maintain himself firmly upon his feet, keep his position, and hold the object steady when I placed my hand or hands upon it, as shown in the figures, just as he was expected to do in the "Umbrella Test."

Now the reader will observe that I have the same advantage in these tests of *position and leverage* as before. The experimenters are under the same disadvantages as to the extreme tension of their bodies, muscles and limbs. They labor under the delusion that they must brace themselves tremendously against some overpowering "Unknown Force" that is going to operate against them. They are like a fierce fire that consumes itself; so they exhaust themselves contending against their own subjective exertions.

As it appears to me now, which is a fact, all I had to do was to divine the direction of their spent energy as they braced against me and fell to, and give way to it, or follow it up. They created the immense momentum that caused the feats, and I gave way to it and allowed it free and full play.

If I had known the principles that produced and controlled the performances then, as I do now, there is absolutely no telling what I could have caused to be accomplished! I believe I could have increased the wonders of my exhibitions tenfold, if my conscience would have allowed me to do so, and if the knowledge of these principles would not have crippled my earnestness and sincerity.

FIGURE 6.

The Attempt to Hold a Cane or Billiard Cue or other Like Object with my Hand upon It.

What I did know, as the phenomena then appeared to me, was that these things were not the result of a sufficient amount of conscious muscular force on my part, to produce such extraordinary manifestations.

Now take the test shown in *figure 6*. I place my hand on the billiard cue or cane at *C*. The experimenter grasps it like a vise at *A* and *B*. I hold my hand there waiting and expecting the "Great Unknown" to come. In the tension of this waiting and expectancy I, unconsciously to a large extent, give more or less of a pressure at *C*. And, mark you, *but a little is ever needed!*

The experimenter, whose quickened nerves and senses are all alert, imagines he feels the oncoming of the "Power." He braces against the slightest indication of an imaginary force. I discern his bracing toward me, and, as I never knew the direction the "Force" would take in its action any more than my subjects did, I give way to this action of the force as I feel it. This giving way on my part throws him forward, and off his balance. He attempts to regain it, and, in doing so, pushes against my hand, which I endeavor to keep in contact with the object. This exertion on his part, instead of regaining his balance, throws him back the other way, in a rebound, as it were, from my touch. He then steps to one side, to the right or to the left. I endeavor to keep up with him. In the effort to keep this contact, I exert enough force to keep him from regaining his balance. He imagines the "Force" has got him in its invincible clutches. He gets disconcerted, loses all self-control and presence of mind, strains his muscles, his body and his limbs to a more terrible tension than ever, but all to no purpose. In doing this he is only aiding me and consuming his own strength. The result is, his wild dance over the stage grows more and more reckless, until finally he lands on the floor or hurls himself into the wings or off the stage, if some one doesn't catch him.

He gets up panting, breathless, wet with perspiration, exhausted, his pulse beating at the rate of 130 a minute, and his respiration 60. I am as cool and calm and fresh as when the test began. *The man has simply made himself do just what he expected the "Mysterious Power" would do!*

There may have been two or three against me in the test, it makes no difference. As viewed by the audience, I have only accomplished the greater wonders. These men have simply contended against one another instead of against me. The great athlete, Prof. Lafflin, in New York, and the world-renowned Japanese Wrestler, Matsada, in Brooklyn, with two or three powerful men to help them, were just as easy to utterly vanquish as any one ordinary man.

*　　*　　*　　*　　*　　*　　*　　*　　*

The chair test, *figure 7*, is accomplished on the same principles, only the positions in holding the chair are a little different, as shown in the cut. The experimenter is requested to hold the chair firmly to his body, grasping it at and A and B maintain his position and keep himself steadily upon his feet when I place my hands upon the chair at C and D. In making this test the experimenter labors under the same disadvantages of position, tension of body, muscles, limbs, etc., as in the last two described, and I have the same advantages of leverage, etc. The *modus operandi* of overcoming the experimenter and keeping the process going, is exactly the same as detailed in the last two experiments.

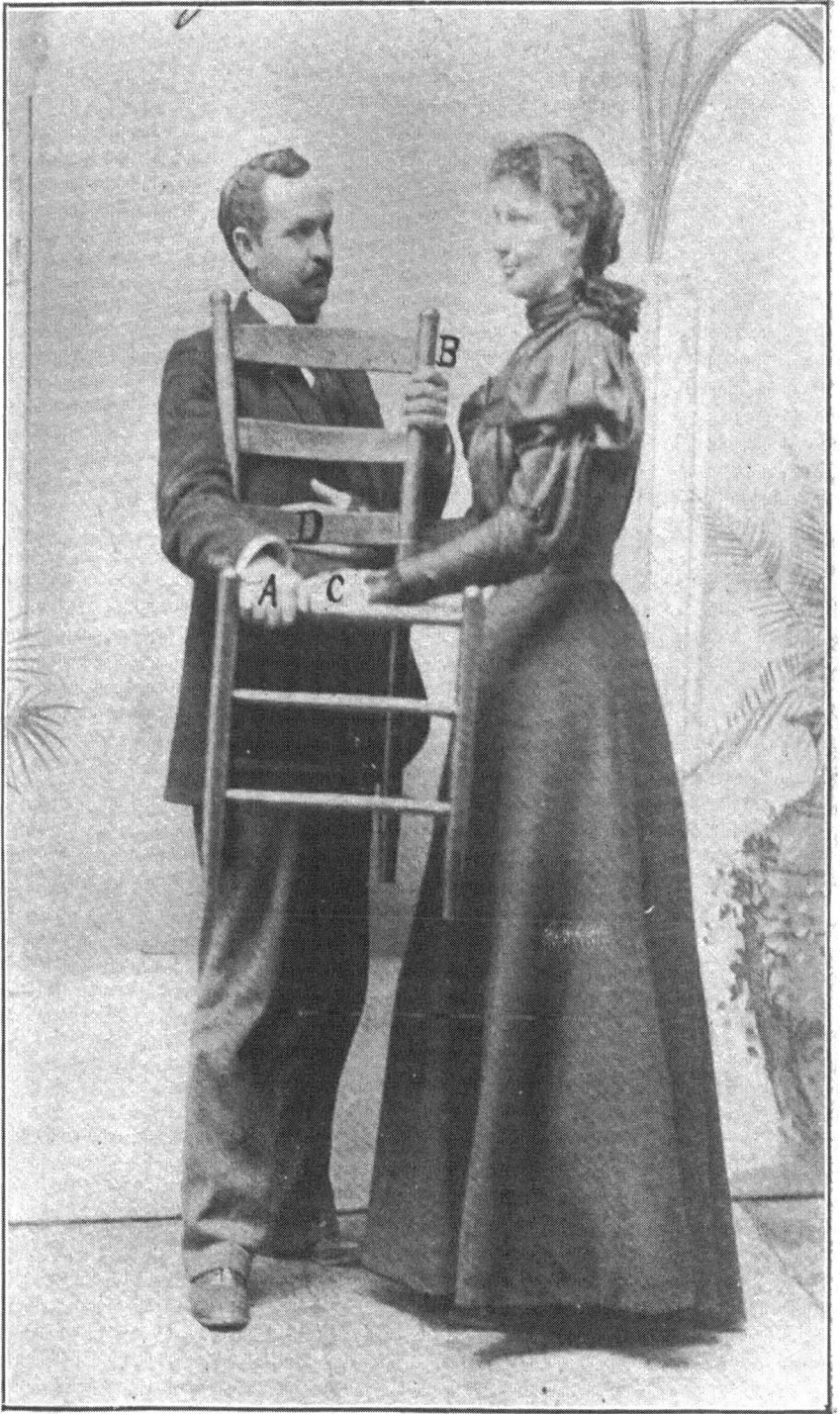

FIGURE 7.

THE ATTEMPT TO HOLD A CHAIR WITH MY HANDS UPON IT.

In making these tests, what pressure I exerted, in first getting the experimenter off his balance, was done so gradually and slowly that it was imperceptible. To prove this, I used to place my hands over those of the experimenters, and they always declared that they felt no appreciable pressure. Doctors who felt my arms said my muscles were not contracted during the tests.

The truth is, I did not comprehend at that time that the small amount of pressure exerted by me had so much to do with accomplishing such remarkable results. For the principles underlying the application of this small force on my part were not understood, nor even realized, by me.

And yet, as remarkable as it may seem, this form of force or pressure was all that was necessary, under the circumstances and in the environments as they then existed, to accomplish these remarkable phenomena. Those experimenting with these tests now can accomplish them, but with the "mystery" all gone, they will not seem so remarkable, nor will success be so easily achieved, or be so convincing. But this will be owing simply to changed conditions and not to changed principles of leverage or mechanical forces. Then, of course, the remarkable tact and knack I acquired in doing these things so often and for so long a time, though acquired unconsciously, must be taken into account. Any novice will labor under disadvantages in doing these things, as he would in anything else.

Then also I got to be an excellent judge of human nature. I could discern the temperaments, idiosyncrasies, delusions and superstitions of a man almost as soon as he came on the stage. I could tell the skeptics from the rank believers at a glance. I learned how to adapt myself to them. Practice produces experience and experience perfects practice, and I had an abundance of both.

* * * * * * * * *

While we were in New York Professor D. L. Dowd, the author of the widely known work on "Physical Culture," visited our exhibition at Wallack's. He is a high authority on all subjects of gymnastics and muscular development. In his book on this subject he devotes several pages, attempting to explain some of my tests, and while in a few instances as I see it now he approaches near the scientific solution, yet, in other respects, he makes a flat failure. No one attempting to perform my feats according to the rules he lays down could ever accomplish one of them.

His book, however, is one of great scientific value on the subject of physical culture and development, and should be in every gymnasium in the country.

But a year or two ago I read an article in one of the enterprising New York papers which came close to the mark. It was a three-column article, but I will quote this special paragraph only:

" 'The truth is, Miss Hurst gets the leverage on you,' a man said to me who had once been hurled heels over head by the 'Georgia Wonder' when she was on the stage, 'and you can't brace yourself. You see she has you to stand just so. You've got to hold things in just a certain way. Then, in my opinion, she gives some sort of imperceptible push or pressure, and you brace, and then she eases up, and you fall to, and then you lose your footing, and the first thing you know you are off you feet and on your head.

" 'I'll tell you it's a great undiscovered principle of *lever-*

age she's got on to. It's somewhat on the same principle as fiddling a bridge down. It's my opinion that whether she knows it or not, she's made some wonderful mechanical discoveries. Acting on these principles she, with *but a minimum of force, overcomes an unreckoned amount of opposition.*' "

The above quotation and the article it was quoted from had much to do with putting me squarely on the right track of investigation.

How those words impressed me: *"She with but a minimum of force overcomes an unreckoned amount of opposition!"*

It used to be wonderful! wonderful! to me, but it's plain enough now in the light of the principles I have discovered and announced.

In all these tests, *the chair, the umbrella, the cane and the billiard cue, and the experimenter's arms and stiffened body, constitute a powerful and ever ready lever, by means of which the slightest force can topple off his balance the strongest man, and keep him so.* Any one can demonstrate this by giving it a fair trial. This principle of leverage, coupled with the other principles I have announced, constitute a full, complete and demonstrable explanation of these wonderful feats. All one has to do to accomplish these things is to exercise a little tact in handling this lever. Of course the subject of the experiment must place himself and the object in the proper position to form the lever. If this is done the test cannot fail. I have recently (at the time of writing this book) made this disclosure to a couple of gentlemen friends, and after the explanation I said to them :

"Now you understand it, and know how it is done. The mystery is all gone. Take this chair and try to force it to the floor."

They exerted all their power, and though they were strong men and knew the principle and *modus operandi* of the test, they could not force the chair to the floor, so long as they observed the conditions.

They struggled at it until they were exhausted, but in vain. After it was over, one of them, who was a very scientific man, said to me:

"You have indeed made a very wonderful discovery in the application of mechanical forces. With your explanation it is as simple as A B C, without it, as inexplicable as the mysterious action of gravitation. And I can hardly say whether it is more wonderful clothed in its former mystery, or reduced to a category of demonstrable mechanical phenomena."

CHAPTER VI.

DEMONSTRATION No. 8.

"The Table Rapping Test," Commonly Termed "Spirit Rapping"—The Production of "Raps" or Mysterious Popping Sounds in and on the Wood of a Table or Other Object.

The reader is referred to chapters 2 and 3 of PART I of this book to acquaint himself with the beginning, circumstances and surroundings of the phenomena to be treated of in this chapter.

My disposition and temperament as a child had much to do with the course I pursued in following up for my own amusement the little incident which produced the first "rap" in the pillow of the bed—which was produced, as before stated, by the *accidental puncture of the feather ticking covering the pillow by a hairpin in my hair.* If there was one feature of my childhood which was more pronounced than any other, it was that I was always full of jokes and pranks. I loved fun almost as well as life itself. My mind at that age seemed to dwell on some form of fun and joke, and I didn't care who the subject of it was.

There was always a "ghost" in every school I attended, and it was a hard one to catch up with. There was always somebody playing off on the teacher, strewing match heads under his feet, gluing him to his chair, etc.

The "ghost" was no respecter of persons. My pranks oftentimes wove themselves about until they took on different aspects from what I had intended.

So when I saw that night in bed the startling effect that first accidental "rap" had on my cousin, who was sleeping with me, I followed it up for my own amusement. To escape detection in carrying on my fun, I thought of placing my feet against the foot-board of the bedstead, having no idea of what I would or could accomplish. I knew if I kept up the manifestation by thrusting the hairpin in the bed-ticking, I would be caught up with. So it was nothing but my love of a joke and my passion for fun that led me to place my feet against the foot-board of the bed, to see if I could produce any sounds from that source. I had no sooner done so and manipulated my feet in a certain way, than popping sounds began to issue out of the wooden piece constituting the foot-board. I saw at once, child as I was, that I had made a discovery. I found that by maintaining a steady, transverse pressure alternating the direction of the pressure at intervals, that the wood emitted popping sounds. Why it did this I did not then know, and could not have explained. The results obtained by this discovery in the production of these "raps" in the wood of the bed, vastly increased the mystery in the minds of those present, and I must confess, mystified me.

I knew that when I placed my feet in certain positions

on the foot-board and gave certain pressures in certain directions, the "raps" came from the wood, but why? I told no one what part I took in the production of these sounds. Nobody ever knew or could discern that I did anything.

During the time I was experimenting with these "raps," I mischievously adopted other methods to deepen the mystery and carry on my childish fun. It is simply astonishing to me now how slyly and dexterously I carried it out. I slyly took garments out of my cousin's trunk, and placed them in other rooms, hanging them on pictures, cornices, etc. Sometimes I would secrete these garments about my person, and then when we were all sitting in a room, would dexterously flirt them across the room on to a picture or chair. My quick movements being unseen by the family, they would be completely mystified by these occurrences. In the same way I tossed pebbles and pieces of sulphur and glasses, etc., about the house. No one ever suspected me for a moment. When my hair was pulled, as related in Chapter 2, Part I, my first impression was that it was my cousin who pulled it; but when she denied it, I at once knew that it was accidentally pulled, and it instantly occurred to me to attribute it to the "Power" and to thus deepen the mystery. In the same sly way, and with the same mischievous motive in view, I tossed hickory nuts about the house and through the rooms—doing this often while the windows were closed, so that these nuts could not be thought to have bounced in through the open windows in falling from the "Electrical Hickory Nut Tree," as this hickory tree had gotten to be called. Under these circumstances no one could possibly account for how these nuts got in the house, and everybody came to have a mysterious awe about this tree.

I did these things with the intention each day of telling the family and having the laugh on them. I deferred doing this day after day, keeping up my fun all the time. In the meantime the "table-rapping" test had been discovered by me, and the wonders connected with other tests had grown to such proportions that I myself was really astounded. For the neighbors having heard of the mysterious occurrences, had come in and begun the test with chairs, etc., and I discovered the existence of the "Power" over objects when held by other people, *and as manifested by them when I was not touching the objects.* The local papers had heard the gossip of the neighbors about these occurrences, and had given these things newspaper notoriety. This was what I had not counted on as a part of my fun, and it put me in quite a dilemma as to what to do.

After these things occurred I decided to say nothing about my having done the things which I had *purposely* done. I knew that the strange action of the "Force" which they had tested and seen was not purposely caused by muscular exertion on my part for in many instances I was not touching the objects. I have never mentioned those childish pranks, which I purposely did, to any one from that day to this, until I decided to make this explanation to the public. In order to make my statement of all occurrences complete, I thought it best to refer to these things which took place at home, but which formed no part of my public exhibition, and which does not affect the explanation of my wonderful performances which took place on the stage.

Of course, these childish pranks at home ought not to, and will not, influence the mind of any one in forming the proper conclusions of the correctness of my "Demonstrations."

During the first week of the occurrence of these things, some one suggested that we try a table, and see if the "raps" would come from that. We did so, and I found that by applying the same method of pressure with the hands, as I did with my feet on the bedstead, the same results were obtained. The same peculiar, weird, muffled, ghost-like sounds issued from the wood of the table. No wonder deluded, superstitious people had been led to attribute these mysterious sounds to "spirits"! They are indeed most supernatural and unaccountable to those not in the secret. At this time I had never heard of "table-rapping" or "spirit-rapping" phenomena. I didn't know there was such a thing. But some of the older witnesses of my performance with the table had heard of these things, and straightway suggested that this was the same manifestation.

When these sounds in the bed and the table first came, I was as much surprised as any one could be, as I had never thought of such a thing. Yet I found that it worked like a charm, and for a few nights I manipulated it, and the developments that came were startling to me. I can now hardly realize that a clever manipulation caused such results. When experimenting with the bed, the popping sounded as though the whole bed was charged with electricity—the steady, even pressure of my feet would give out one sound, and the gentle relaxing of the pressure would produce a different but equally strange sound. These sounds would not be confined to any particlar part of the bed, but came from all parts, because the pressure as exerted by me affected all parts.   While it was a wonder to me, yet realizing that in some way my manipulation was producing the sounds, it, instead of frightening me, as it did my little home audiences of neighbors and friends, amused me very much indeed.   I must say, however, that the whole development, from the starting point to the conclusion, was more of a surprise to me than to any one else.

When I look back over the whole thing now, it is to my mind most wonderful.   To think that I alone—a mere child—so successfully carried out these phenomena, and how everything conspired to aid me, and how all these developments came within a few days' time—things so unthought of and unheard of by me—I find that I lack the language and the talent to portray my feelings or properly describe the phenomena.

I have had numbers of people time and again to beg me to introduce this table-rapping test in my public performances, but I never would do so.   My management, while I was on the stage, pleaded with me to do so, but I refused peremptorily, and without giving any reasons.   But my reason was that I knew that an imperceptible, but at the same time conscious, manipulation on my part produced the phenomena, and I would not practice a deception on my audiences, even though, as a girl, I did not understand the nature or the intricate solution of the problem; while, in my other stage tests, I knew that I produced but a very infinitesimal part of the cause, and that other wonderful forces and principles, human and mechanical, unknown to me in their method and nature, were the prime and efficient cause.

FIGURE 8.

THE WEIRD TABLE RAPPING TEST, COMMONLY TERMED "SPIRIT-RAPPING."

Since leaving the stage, and while engaging myself more or less for these years in the investigations of my public tests with a view to explaining them, if I could ever get my consent to do so, I have also experimented with and studied the one under consideration, and am satisfied that I have arrived at a solution of all "table-rapping" or so-called "spirit-rapping."

The position to be taken in sitting at a table to produce these raps is not arbitrary. The experimenter, or the so-called "medium," may sit on one side or at either end. But sometimes a table will give out raps only from one certain position or pivot of manipulation, while another table will respond from any or all positions. The "medium" soon discovers these points of peculiarity in tables, and adapts himself or herself accordingly.

If the raps do not come from one position, they give some mysterious excuse about the necessity of trying another. Neither is the position of the hands on the table arbitrary. The usual position, I believe, is to place the hands flat on the cover of the table, palm downwards, as shown in *figure 8*, at *A and B*.

Or the hands may lie longitudinally along the edges of the table at each end. Or any other position may be found to answer as well, according to the construction of the table.

Every table has joints and mortices where it is put together, at the junction of the legs and cross-beams, and also on top where the pieces of the boards forming the cover come together. These unions on the top are shown in *Figure 8*, by the dotted lines on cover. Now the looser these joints fit both in the legs, cross-pieces and cover, the better and the easier are the results obtained. Also the

17 l

thinner and drier—that is, the more *seasoned*—the boards
forming the top are, the more satisfactory are the results.
I defy any so-called "Medium" to get a "rap" from a damp,
moist table, where the joints and unions are firmly and
solidly swollen together, especially if the table is strongly
built and the covering made of thick, solid boards. No
so-called "Spirit" can manifest itself by any "rap" on such
a table as this; and if this phenomenon is the result of a
"spirit" force, why should the construction of a table have
anything to do with it?

Now in a table with a cover of thin boards, these "raps"
occur in various parts of the table *in and on the wooden
boards forming the cover* and in the joints and mortices.
They seem to issue *out of the wood itself* and from a multiplicity of points. They appear not to be confined to any
particular joints or crevices. Sometimes the "raps" have
a muffled, hollow, unlocated sound, and again clear and
resonant. They take on quite a variety of sounds. With
a well *seasoned*, thin-top table, I have had them sound like
a blow from a hammer, and on one occasion I caused the top
of the table to burst off. And yet the manipulation of the
force required to accomplish these things is so slow, gradual
and unseen, that the shrewdest investigator could detect
absolutely no exertion on my part. It is not discernible
in my arms or hands, and yet with some tables a considerable amount of pressure is necessary. A month or two ago
I told the secret of it to a friend of mine, and he has acquired almost as much tact in doing it as I have.

Well, now say we have the proper table—and the
"Mediums" always have or select their own tables—and
we take our position as shown. You will observe that the

dotted lines on the top that the boards and joints of the cover run transversely to our body and hands, and not straight out from us. By taking this position with the hands at *A* and *B* we get a remarkable *purchase* on these cross-sections, joints and unions of the table, and by a very gradual pressure of the hands in opposite directions, one toward *C* and one toward *D*, we cause an imperceptible strain in the joints and unions of the parts of the table. This gradual pressure, when properly exercised, is absolutely indiscernible to any one looking on. Now when you have put on enough pressure to cause this strain—and it can and must be done without moving the hands and arms perceptibly or the body of the table at all—then the rap in and on the wood comes. Then when you hear this rap, you must just as gradually relax the pressure, and allow the strain to go out, and the raps will keep coming all the while. You then begin and go through the same process again, and the popping sound will continue *ad infinitum.* If it is found that these sounds do not come from this effort on one side of the table, try the other, and then the ends, for often a table is so constructed that you cannot strain the joints and cover sections from one direction of pressure so as to produce the phenomena, whereas you can from another.

Now when this imperceptible strain takes place, it results in releasing the minute adhesions of the wood fiber, glue, paint, etc., forming the immediate, hidden union and mortices of the parts of the table, boards, etc., and this dissolution and snapping asunder of these minute parts gives out *in and on and through the wood* the peculiar, weird sounds that are heard. The sounds will often come from all parts of the table, and can scarcely be located. It seems to have no relation to the joints and crevices. Sometimes it will be found that the pressure of one hand only will accomplish the same results.

When one has acquired the tact in carrying on the process, one can cause the raps to come just when desired, for the purpose of mystifying people, answering questions, etc. In answering questions and imparting information, etc., by means of the raps, one must exercise plenty of common sense and judgment, and must bring to one's aid a good knowledge of human nature. Besides, the person who wants the information, must ask the questions, do the counting, etc.

We agree upon a code of signals or a kind of sign language. Say there will be one rap for "no," two for "yes," and three for " don't know," etc. The questioner desires for instance, some message to be spelled out from the alphabet. He calls the letters and when he gets to the desired letter, the table must rap. The letters as they are rapped out form words, and the words sentences.

In getting at dates he counts, and the table raps at the correct numbers. One must be able to judge by the questioner's tone of voice, inflection, etc., as well as from the expression of his countenance, when to cause the rap. I very seldom made a failure when experimenting for my amusement and to satisfy the curiosity of friends and acquaintances.

I could almost invariably tell by observing the questioner's tone of voice—inflection, slight hesitation, expression of countenance, etc.—when to make the rap come. I have thus mystified people beyond expression, when they prevailed upon me to give them this test. When I did give it I never made any claims to it as an occult phenomenon, nor did I explain to any one the process of doing it. I could not then have explained it as I can now, but I did not produce it on the stage for the reasons heretofore given.

It was those same principles that caused the raps to come in and on the foot-board of the bed, which I have described.

Now in this demonstration which I have here given so fully and minutely, so that any one with a little tact and practice can do it, we have the whole explanation of that wide-spread superstition known as "Spirit-Table-Rapping." There is absolutely no doubt of it. It is all based on superstition in the believers, and on fraud and mechanical manipulation by the "mediums," who feast upon the delusions they create and maintain in the minds of their dupes. In principle, it is a plain case of mechanical cause and effect.

I discovered it accidentally and sought out the explanation, and I can now duplicate the performance, in this respect, of any so-called "medium." I can produce this phenomenon before people not acquainted with this explanation, and nine out of ten of them will ascribe it to some occult cause. A few may refer it to magnetic or electric origin, but the great majority will term it "odic" or "psychic," or "spiritistic." I have noted this tendency so often in the minds of people that I know whereof I speak. It was just this knowledge of such wide-spread delusion on such subjects that caused me to abandon the stage and constrained me to prepare and publish this volume.

I felt that this disclosure was a duty I owed the public in the light of my past history, and that the knowledge I possessed on the subjects treated would be of great benefit to some people. It was this consciousness of a duty to be performed that caused me to undergo the notoriety of bringing this subject again before the public. I greatly preferred the sweet, domestic calm, peace and solitude of my home-life to any notoriety or emolument I might gain by the publication of this volume. But outside of and above all other considerations, I realized as I grew older that the consciousness of a duty faithfully performed is in itself the greatest reward.

If this volume will accomplish the purposes I had in view in writing it, then it may appear that after all the "Georgia Wonder" was not sent forth in vain.

CHAPTER VII.

A FAREWELL TALK WITH MY READERS.

A Few Lessons Taught by the Power—The Final Work of the Georgia Wonder.

When I was on the stage it was always astonishing to me how easily people were deluded, and led away from the path of reason, and how prone they were to allow themselves to become victims of their imagination and superstition. The wonderful record in PART I of this book proves this conclusively.

In so far as I have been instrumental in fostering, aiding or producing superstitious ideas at a time when I could not satisfactorily explain what appeared to be such a great mystery, just so far have I desired in the writing of this book to correct these false ideas by reducing the "Great Secret" to a series of natural, demonstrable phenomena.

I hope this little volume will impress upon the minds of the people everywhere that there *is and must be reason in all things;* that there is nothing in this world, however mysterious and seemingly inexplicable, which cannot be explained along the line of cause and effect.

That people should always remember that there must be

a *tangible cause for every tangible effect*, and that it is
there whether they detect it or not. I hope this book will
fortify the minds of one and all, to some extent at least,
against anything and everything that smacks of the unreal!
I have felt more or less of a burden resting on me ever
since I began to realize how superstitious ideas were growing out of my performances, and I some time ago made up
my mind that this burden would not be fully lifted until I
had disclosed to the world the contents of this book.

    *   *   *   *   *   *

If there is any person or newspaper or journal or public print of any kind disposed to criticize me harshly, after
having acquainted themselves with the disclosures in this
volume, then I will willingly and cheerfully bear such
criticism, feeling that a sacred duty conscientiously performed is a sufficient reward to me. Every one of cultured
conscience, it seems to me, must commend my course *as a
woman* in giving to the world this explanantion of the
Great Secret—so if they cast upon me cruel criticism or
harsh blame for what I did years ago when a girl, they must
remember that they hurl them at the head of a *fourteen-
year-old girl*, who, having employed innocently and ignorantly certain principles in mechanics and leverage, which
she could not then comprehend, used these to astonish the
world, and then to make money out of a wondering and
deluded continent!

I think this volume gives an idea to what extent the
public mind of this country is imbued with superstition,
and controlled by delusion and imagination and a care-
ful reading will convince you that this applies not only
to the so-called ignorant classes, but to scientists, savants

and literateurs. Nor does there appear to be any difference in this respect between one section of the country and another. The North, East, South and West are all alike. There seems to be something in our society or nature or education, I know not which, that makes our people—not the ignorant class, simply, but the learned and erudite—subject to superstitious ideas, and that places them at the mercy of any form of mysterious phenomena which they happen not to understand. It seems that the safeguard of reason within us has been weakened, and its protective power over our minds rendered largely imbecile, on account of our disregard of its laws.

I leave to philosophers and thinkers to decide, *whether it is safe and right and best for the race in the long run to encourage the people to believe in, or to admit as provable, any so-called class of facts which are at variance with the known system of nature, contrary to the laws of our reason, and that cannot be explained along the eternally established line of cause and effect!* The record in this book, and it is a true one, shows that the people everywhere were ready to accept and admit any unproved, occult theory, or "anything" concerning the phenomena manifested through me, which was put forth. It made no difference what sort of wonderful claims theorists made for it, many were willing to admit them.

Of course there were some skeptics, or what might be termed "Realists," who clung to the theory of a natural interpretation, but these "skeptics" were few, and the believers in the "occult theory" made it hot for them. If they essayed to express doubt on the subject, they were given no showing, but were hooted and hissed off the stage, and at times, when they persisted in attempting to express themselves, a riot in the audience seemed imminent. But, unlike my audiences, my consideration and sympathy for the skeptics were great, because I realized that they were entitled to a hearing, and did not deserve such harsh treatment. I think I can truthfully state, however, that usually after my performances, when people had seen my tests, not one in five hundred were skeptical on the point of the "occult nature" of my "power."

It was a knowledge of these facts and of this superstitious belief of the people, that made me so anxious after arriving at the solution to give this explanation and demonstration of my "Force."

While all must admit that my feats were marvelous, and especially so in their effect upon the people, yet one of the most wonderful things about it all was the way I, when a mere child, unconsciously, or rather ignorantly, got into the methods of applying such extraordinary power, and how I exercised the phenomenal tact by which the tests were so successfully carried out. This must be admitted, when it is considered that of the tens of thousands who witnessed and tested the "Power," no one ever solved the "Great Secret." Every one of my tests was done on the open stage with spectators and investigators all around me, and in the brightest and best light that gas and electricity could afford.

If this book will do no more than fortify the minds of the people against all superstition, it will justify my having written it, and will be sufficient excuse for the existence of such a volume. In this way the "Georgia Wonder" may accomplish a lasting benefit after all, and the "Power" prove more of a blessing than was ever dreamed of.

My performances began at age fourteen and ended at age sixteen.

My last performances were among my greatest successes from every point of view. As stated before, I exhibited for the last time at Knoxville, Tennessee, to an immense audience. Here we turned away as many as were able to get into the house. The excitement was intense. People were wild over my exhibition. But this night (as I narrated in the last chapter of PART I), I made up my mind, should be my last appearance before the public. As I have before stated, I saw the harm (and had seen it for some time) that my exhibitions were doing. I had reached an age even at sixteen where I saw this. I determined to call a halt. I have never given a performance from that day to this, either in public or private, except recently, and then to demonstrate that my "explanation" as given in this book is absolutely true. Until recently I would not discuss the subject with people, but the problem was always in my mind. For I have seen, year by year, the evil effects in the public mind. I have felt more and more, as the years went by, and I understood more thoroughly the nature of the "Power," that I owed the public a duty. The "explanation" as it came to me more clearly weighed upon my conscience.

I have been advised not to make this explanation. My reply has been, that if the performance of a sacred duty merits any unkind criticism, I am more than able to bear it. This burden will be less by far than that resting on me of "the Great Secret."

THE END.

72968841R00168

Made in the USA
San Bernardino, CA
30 March 2018